BY THE AUTHOR:

The Only Way to Cross

Dark Brown Is the River

S/S Norway

Olympic/Titanic

Liners to the Sun

Tribute to a Queen

From Song to Sovereign

Cunard: 150 Glorious Years

Monarch of the Seas

Majesty of the Seas

Safe Return Doubtful

Crossing & Cruising

Legend of the Seas

Under Crown & Anchor

Splendour of the Seas

Grandeur of the Seas

Grand Princess

Sun Princess

Dawn Princess

Titanic Survivor

Cruise Savvy

Century

Queen Mary 2

Normandie

France/Norway

TITANIC TRAGEDY

JOHN MAXTONE-GRAHAM

TITANIC TRAGEDY

A NEW LOOK AT THE LOST LINER

W. W. NORTON & COMPANY

NEW YORK · LONDON

Titanic Tragedy

John Maxtone-Graham

Printed in the United States
First Edition

Manufacturing by Courier Westford
Composed in Stellar, Electra, and Metro
Book design by Robert L. Wiser, Silver Spring, MD

Library of Congress Cataloging-in-Publication Data

Maxtone-Graham, John.
Titanic tragedy : a new look at the lost liner / John Maxtone-Graham. — 1st ed.
p. cm.
Includes bibliographical references and index.
ISBN 978-0-393-08240-1 (hardcover)
1. Titanic (Steamship) 2. Shipwrecks—North Atlantic Ocean. I. Title.
G530.T6M366 2012
910.9163'4—dc23 2011030936

W. W. Norton & Company
500 Fifth Avenue, New York, NY 10110
www.wwnorton.com

W. W. Norton & Company Ltd.
Castle House, 75/76 Wells Street, London, WIT 3QT

1 2 3 4 5 6 7 8 9 0

Endpapers: A rare photograph showing *Olympic* and *Titanic* together at Harland and Wolff. The date is 6 March 1912. *Titanic* had been in the Thompson Graving Dock but inbound *Olympic*, with a propeller needing repair, necessitated the second vessel's displacement. As a result, both vessels are parked alongside their fitting-out jetties, *Titanic* on the left, *Olympic* on the right. What looks like smoke emerging from *Titanic*'s fourth dummy funnel is actually steam. The giant floating crane Hercules can be seen just to the right of *Olympic*'s fourth funnel. **(Tom McCluskie private collection)**

Dedicated

to the memory of

Walter Lord

1917–2002

CONTENTS

PREFACE

Walter Lord's final book was The Night Lives On, *published* in 1986, in which he refined details from his *Titanic* classic, *A Night to Remember,* of three decades earlier—undoubtably his most memorable book.

I recall several conversations with Walter while he was in the throes of completing that last volume. To the end, deadlines dismayed him: "I am not ready," he grumbled more than once, "to let this manuscript go." He later described his book as "an old man's recall of some *Titanic* loose ends that need clearing up." In fact, at sixty-nine, he was barely old but doubtless felt prematurely aged by the insidious effects of Parkinson's.

Now, in my early eighties, I should recapitulate, amplifying observations from past books, articles, catalogues, and lectures that dwelt on White Star's notorious loss. I am less concerned with clearing up loose ends than with creating what might be described as historical stepping-stones, documenting events and episodes leading up to and emanating from the disaster.

Since Marconi and Morse remain unquestionably *Titanic*'s most pivotal players, we should start with their sublime inventions, which permitted communication between ships. Thanks to that miraculous network we can eavesdrop on worrisome dispatches crackling through the night of 15 April 1912, alerting nearby masters to the unfolding tragedy.

A staunch supporting player was Thomas Andrews, Harland and Wolff's beloved naval architect, who died in the wreck. He designed both of the *Olympic*-class vessels and we shall visit the Belfast yard where they were wrought.

Southampton's capacious Ocean Dock, excavated from 1908 to 1911 and recently revived for passenger use, was created specifically for the *Olympic*-class giants. As starting point of *Titanic*'s maiden and only crossing, its berth no. 44 remains holy ground.

Then I will turn to the jarring realities of lifeboat evacuation as well as the testimony of survivors I interviewed four decades ago. We shall board rescue vessel *Carpathia*, diverted from her Mediterranean cruise to race north for *Titanic*.

After some crew memorials have been examined an unique finale: seven previously unpublished *Titanic* parodies composed by Walter Lord.

Titanic's foundering remains the world's most compelling maritime saga. It should come as no surprise that among the *New York Times* store's best-selling merchandise are models of the lost vessel. Moreover, centenary's achievement will ensure a continuing avalanche of books, articles, television programs, films, paintings, and, inevitably, controversy. Succeeding generations of obsessives will surely take our place.

Chronological milestones always trigger new outpourings. As the April 2012 centenary approaches, old and/or novel theories will surface, from metallurgists preoccupied with brittle fracture or flawed rivets to critics of imperfect naval architecture; from those appalled by the lifeboat shortage or the preponderant toll of immigrant deaths to those outraged by desecration of a tomb; from those condemning Captain Smith's reckless speed to that unending dispute over *Californian*'s adjacency to or distance from *Titanic*.

In a letter to Captain's Smith's daughter Melinda, Walter encapsulated his intent for shaping *A Night to Remember*.

I just want to recreate the night the *Titanic* went down so that anybody can picture exactly what it was like. I want to recapture all the little incidents and details. I want to preserve all the drama, excitement and courage that blended with the ice and the stars to make this night so utterly unforgettable.

That was the master's imperishable formula for conjuring up the tragedy's dramatic minutiae. *A Night to Remember* rekindled the world's *Titanic* awareness, thanks to its author's innovative and flawless reportage.

Walter Lord died on Sunday, 19 May 2002, aged eighty-four. A close friend, colleague, and mentor, this volume is dedicated to his beloved memory.

My eternal gratitude, as always, to my dear wife and cabinmate Mary, whose computer expertise is forever on call, who hears every chapter first and whose interest, compassion, good humor, bountiful spirit, and wisdom enrich this maritime historian's life completely.

John Maxtone-Graham
South Atlantic, March 2011

ACKNOWLEDGMENTS

First thanks, as always, are due my Norton editor, Jim Mairs, for staunch and unstinting support, his most capable and dependable right-hand, Austin O'Driscoll, and the incredibly talented Maryland designer Robert Wiser.

Britain's incomparable maritime artist Robert Lloyd has once again provided a hauntingly apropos cover painting, the first *Titanic* he has ever attempted. My longtime colleague Wayne Mazzotta has contributed two beautifully rendered period maps, typographically enriched by Nick Burkett.

There is, thankfully, no shortage of ship buffs around the world, including a corps of incredibly knowledgeable *Titanic* experts I have known and relied on for years. My profound gratitude to historians Don Lynch and John Eaton for their unending help with all manner of details about the disaster. California maritime artist and *Titanic* expert Ken Marschall proved, once again, a gold mine of extraordinary arcana. What a privilege to tap into their combined expertise, so freely given and generously shared.

I was ably assisted by a dependable ad hoc committee of wireless specialists, including Americans Paul Bock, Parks Stephenson, fellow U.S. marine William Hadrys, and, from the Netherlands, the late and lamented Edward De Groot. Their encyclopedic knowledge about early wireless telegraphy in general and *Titanic*'s wireless installation in particular was invaluable. Cornishman Bill Behenna provided useful Poldhu input.

I am equally grateful for the helpful collaboration of Edward and Karen Kamuda of the Titanic Historical Society, that irreplaceable American organization in Massachusetts. Closer to home, Manhattan's Jenny Lawrence was enormously helpful on a variety of fronts, Walter Lord's oeuvre in particular. Unlimited access to Christopher Lee's original *Olympic* and *Titanic* deck plans was enormously helpful.

For details about the Ocean Dock, I profited from the combined knowledge of several officials of Associated British Ports, the body that administrates seventeen United Kingdom ports, Southampton among them. Recently retired marine administration manager Ron Hancock proved an irreplaceable resource, so too Glen Gardner, Lorraine Nottley, and, most especially, Kate Finnegan, my indefatigable guide to so much of Southampton's history of a century ago.

In addition to the late Edward De Groots's wireless expertise, I am indebted to him for his permission to reproduce, for the first time anywhere, Walter Lord's seven parodic anniversary letters shared with fellow author Leslie Reade during the 1970s.

Engineer Captain Peter Mansfield, RN retired, together with Cunard chief engineer Ronnie Keir were enormously helpful. So, too, as always, was retired Cunard commodore and old friend Ron Warwick.

As my host and guide in Belfast, Tom McCluskie shepherded me around what remains of Harland and Wolff's original infrastructure, most eloquently the surviving Thompson Graving Dock. As not only a fellow maritime historian but also a former Harland and Wolff employee, his familiarity with the yard's history is unmatched.

I was immeasurably assisted by the staff of Greenwich's National Maritime Museum. Its James Caird reading room is remarkable, a treasure trove beautifully administrated and preserved.

Alphabetically listed thanks must be conveyed to Winthrop Aldrich, *QM2* retired captain Nick Bates, Leon Fitzgerald, Vera Gillespie, Sir Alistair Horne, David Hutchings, Anthony Inglis, Michael Jedd, Trian Koutoufaris, Stuart Lodington, Murray MacDonald, the late William Sloper, and William Thacher. Any omissions are most sincerely regretted.

TITANIC TRAGEDY

CHAPTER I

THE WIRELESS MIRACLE

Would you call a friend from half across the world?
If you'll let us have his name and town and state,
You shall see and hear your cracking question hurled
Across the arch of heaven while you wait.

Rudyard Kipling, from "The Secret of the Machines"

· · · — — — · · · *"Distress" signal* (Notzeichen).
This is to be repeated by a ship in distress until all other stations have stopped working.

The Electrician, 5 May 1905

Surviving passengers and crew of Titanic *owed their lives to* two giants of transatlantic innovation, Samuel Morse and Guglielmo Marconi. Their combined achievements from opposite sides of the ocean established an incredible communication linkage, connecting continents, countries, and ships. Not surprisingly, their names have entered the language: there is the verb coinage to Morse and millions of Marconigrams have been dispatched and delivered. Hence they become obligatory subjects of this opening chapter.

Samuel Finley Breese Morse was born in Charlestown, Massachusetts, on 27 April 1791, son of a fiery Calvinist pastor. Unlike Marconi, young Morse proved a dedicated and successful student. After completion of his schooling at Philips Academy in Andover, he was admitted to Yale, graduating Phi Beta Kappa in 1810 at the age of nineteen. A talented artist, Samuel elected to support himself by painting portraits, a decision only grudgingly accepted by his father. He traveled to England, remaining there to study throughout the War of 1812. After he returned to the United States portrait commissions began to accrue, including one from the White House. Former president John Adams sat for him, as did the Marquis de Lafayette and several members of Congress.

Morse might have remained a successful portraitist but for the tragic loss of his beloved wife Lucretia, about whose mortal illness he learned too late to reach her bedside. Shattered by her death without him and by the idea that she might have thought him indifferent, he abandoned palette and canvas, devoting himself instead to the infant science of telegraphy. Aboard a westbound ship sailing from England, he had struck up a chance acquaintance with fellow passenger Dr. Charles Jackson, doctor and inventor, who suggested that a message might be sent quickly along a wire. That a method of fast communication should preoccupy the grieving widower was scarcely surprising. Morse perfected both a transmitter and receiver and, most important, an alphabetical code, the first that enabled signals to be sent along a wire via electrical impulses. Exactly like Marconi to come, he battled rival patent holders of his time; several minds were working along the same lines.

Just as wireless would, in a sense, predate today's texting mania, so Morse foreshadowed our computers' reliance on binary reduction. Rather than integers 1 and 2, Morse's binary symbols were short dots and, of two times longer duration, dashes, the *dits* and *dahs* of which his invented telegraphese was constructed. Perfected in 1840, different dot/dash arrangements were devised for every letter of the alphabet as well as for ten numerals and some punctuation marks. While no letter was assigned more than four symbols, some had only one: E a single dot, T a single dash. A boasted dot/dash and N the reverse, dash/dot. Although H had four dots, no letter was represented by four dashes. Only for the ten integers did Morse expand his symbol count from four to five, two with a decimal whiff: the number 5 was represented by five dots and 0 by five dashes. It is probably safe to say that those ostensibly unfamiliar with Morse's code know at least three of its letters well: S and O of SOS as well as the three dots and a dash for v, anachronistically conveyed by the clarion opening bars of Beethoven's Fifth Symphony.

Identified first as American Morse code, it became famous as plain Morse code, flourishing as a vital government, newspaper, and railway convenience. Parades of telegraph poles festooned with wires became the accompanying concomitant of every track stitching America, piggybacking on the railroaders' right-of-way to ensure instant, failsafe communication along every line.

Many of those railway telegraphers fell victim to what was described by medicos as telegraphers' paralysis or, by its victims, as "glass arm." After months of constant repetition, Morse signals were more than tapped; the required hand motion became an insistent pressing or thumping that provoked the earliest instance of the carpal tunnel syndrome that afflicts many of today's computer keyboard operators.

To alleviate the condition, late in the nineteenth century, the J. H. Bunnell Company perfected an improved sending key christened the "sideswiper." Moving only fractionally left and right, operators could transmit dots and dashes without suffering the cumulative abuse of vertical key operation.

If Morse pioneered telegraphic communication over wires, establishing the same communication without wires would emerge as Marconi's history-making achievement. Although that wireless technology was the product of several rival minds, Guglielmo Marconi has been acknowledged as the first not only to perfect it but also to capitalize on it.

Born at Palazzo Marescalchi, Bologna, Italy, on 25 April 1874, he was the second son of a mixed European marriage: Italian Giuseppe Marconi had wed Irish Annie Jameson, granddaughter of the founder of Jameson's distillery. Throughout the course of his sometimes slapdash education, Marconi enjoyed his mother's unwavering support and, too often, the undisguised antagonism of his father.

Signora Marconi set the tone for her second son's upbringing by taking Guglielmo, aged three, for a long stay in Britain. When they returned three years later, her husband insisted that the boy, fluent in English, settle down and learn Italian. He was enrolled in a Florentine boarding school where, because of his Anglicization, he was bullied and ridiculed. The only profitable legacy of that unhappy interval was the friendship of fellow student Luigi Solari, who would become a lifelong colleague and employee.

A disappointing student, young Marconi's overriding interest was electricity. In 1893, with his mother's blessing and his father's reluctant consent, he set up an amateur laboratory in the family's Villa Griffone attic. Marconi was a born tinkerer; among his earliest inventions was a primitive still, followed by transformation of his cousin Daisy's sewing machine into a mechanical spit.

But however the boy dabbled, Marconi *père* disapproved. Young Guglielmo's manners and attitude were abysmal. Summoned to meals from his attic hideaway, he arrived late and, at table, either ignored or irritated his father. After he inadvertently broke some precious family crockery, Giuseppe Marconi became so enraged that wherever he encountered his son's experiments he would trash them.

In 1887 Heinrich Hertz had discovered that electrical energy could be radiated through space via what were described as radio waves. By then, Marconi's father had faced reality and dispatched Guglielmo to Livorno's Technical Institute to study physics and electricity. There, he befriended a retired blind telegrapher who, in return for Marconi's reading aloud to him, taught the young man Morse code. Later, back in the winter chill of his attic laboratory, Marconi decided to adapt Hertz's radio waves to the transmission of wireless messages. By installing a Branly coherer, a reception device, he effected a miraculous transmission without wires, activating a little battery-powered buzzer 30 feet (9 meters) away.

That Marconi was not accepted at the University of Bologna further infuriated his father. Yet again—in a consistent familial dynamic—doting Annie intervened and persuaded senior professor Augusto Righi to grant her son the use of some of the university's facilities.

Over ensuing months, Marconi's daily struggle was extending the range of his transmissions. Out on the villa's terrace, with an improved coherer combining nickel and silver for greater sensitivity, he did better. He tried something different every day—metal slabs originally buried in the ground became aboveground aerials. The triumphant waving of a signal flag across local fields indicated ever more distant reception. His radio waves, Marconi discovered, went over but not through intervening hills; line of sight was not essential but ground obstructions could sometimes intervene. Even his father offered grudging respect, urging his son to submit his invention to officials of the Italian navy; they evinced no interest.

Once again, Marconi and his mother departed for the United Kingdom, her son carrying a black japanned metal box containing his most precious equipment. In London Annie's nephew Henry Jameson-Davies helped settle them in a house on Bayswater Road. He also strongly recommended that the young inventor submit a patent application that was finally awarded on 2 June 1896. Marconi settled on a name for his company, Marconi Wireless and Signal. An Italian investor offered him 300,000 lire for the rights to his invention but Marconi turned him down.

His most fruitful London connection came three years later, after a successful interview with William Preece, the gentle bearded Welshman who was chief electrical engineer of Britain's general post office, a man enviably well connected with numerous government departments.

After delivering two highly complimentary papers on Marconi's achievements, Preece arranged for a wireless demonstration in

London on the roof of the general post office building in St Martins-le-Grand. A signal was successfully transmitted to a receiver atop another post office building in Queen Victoria Street. The demonstration was a resounding success; those present were amazed that Marconi's radio waves reached their destination despite intervening buildings.

In Italy, Marconi's longest transmission had been just under a mile. Working with improved antennas, dogged increments of achievement followed in the UK. By March 1897 Marconi was transmitting signals for 3.7 miles (6 kilometers) across Salisbury Plain. Two months later, the first wireless communication was dispatched across open water, nearly four miles across the Bristol Channel. Rather than Morse's awestruck "What hath God wrought?" Marconi's first overwater dispatch began with the accidental preliminary: "Are you ready?"

In the summer of 1897 Marconi conducted a demonstration for Italian officials in La Spezia's San Bartolomeo naval dockyard. There, he achieved history's first transmission from ship to shore, sending from the battleship *San Martino* to a dockyard receiver. Though impressed, the navy made no overt offer and Marconi returned to London empty-handed. Meanwhile, in Germany, rival inventor Adolf Slaby was also experimenting with overwater transmissions at Kiel.

Marconi continued extending his wireless range. Ireland and England were experimentally connected in 1898 and he managed a cross-Channel dispatch the following year. A Marconi demonstration in New York included coverage of an America's Cup race off Sandy Hook. After the New York Yacht Club's *Columbia* trounced Thomas Lipton's *Shamrock*, news of the victory was dispatched ashore via a transmitter set up in a disused cloak room aboard the steamship *Ponce*. Successfully received at a New Jersey shore station in Navesink, the news was then forwarded by telephone to Manhattan's

Thirty-fourth Street. Highly impressed, the U.S. Navy debated replacing its carrier pigeon flocks with Marconi's invention.

Marconi was tall and slim, handsome and eternally restless, a driven man always intent on his next breakthrough. Throughout an often unhappy childhood, adolescence, early adulthood, and, indeed, entire life, his overriding preoccupation was perfecting and improving wireless reception and transmission, a consuming idée fixe. Success, both scientific and financial, drove him relentlessly, to the exclusion of all else—parents, siblings, wife, children, or home. It was a quest that condemned him, in those earliest, experimental years, to continual discomfort and isolation, yet the man throve on it. Bleak, desolate coastlines became Marconi's inevitable stock in trade. He was equally drawn to sea on storm-ravaged vessels. Once, afloat in a punishing Channel gale, Marconi toiled contentedly aboard a pitching chartered tug with a foot of water sloshing about its saloon, its master and crew miserable but the tireless inventor delighted that all his wireless elements were functioning perfectly.

Just after the turn of the century Marconi brought off a splendid coup in St. John's, Newfoundland, Canada's easternmost port. Its harbor is a kind of child's dream, a rectangle of protected water achieved by sea entry through narrows flanked by towering, rock-girt eminences. The taller of the two, northernmost Signal Hill, rears 465 feet (140 meters) above the sea.

To maintain secrecy he told his Canadian hosts that he was attempting to make wireless contact with various Cunarders at sea, but his actual goal was far more ambitious. Atop Signal Hill, he and a team of helpers flew an airborne antenna suspended beneath a kite. Both kite and antenna swooped and bobbed erratically in the gale.

Later, aerials were attached to hydrogen-filled balloons, 14 feet in diameter. Temperatures fell, winds raged, and working conditions were appalling. The 11 December entry of assistant George Kemp's pocket notebook said it all. One can almost hear its pages fluttering in that constant gale as, with gloved hands, Kemp documented each experiment.

> Put balloon up in a strong breeze and lost it 3 P.M. when it was blown away. Mr Marconi trying to get [illegible] during the time balloon was up on various Receivers, calling me at interval.

The following day, a kite was sent aloft again.

> Lost first kite with two 500-foot wires after being up for an hour. Then put up another with [illegibile] 500-foot wire which kept it up 3 hours and appeared to find life good.

Despite his antenna's fearful gyrations, Marconi received a just-audible signal dispatched not from a Cunarder but from his shore station at Poldhu atop the Cornish cliffs, 2,170 miles (almost 3500 kilometers) distant. It was not a bona fide message, merely repeated transmissions of the letter S—three dots—a telegraphed mantra automatically cranked out for hours on end. Just after noon on 12 December 1901, three sequences of those precious *dits* from Cornwall were indisputably plucked from the ether via Marconi's flying receptor high over St. John's. Perpetual copyright controversies dogged Marconi's early career. Nikola Tesla, an American claimant as wireless inventor, argued that to achieve his feat the Italian had stolen no less than seventeen of his—Tesla's—patents.

Undeterred, Marconi continued. Other experiments tested continuous reception aboard a vessel at sea. Aboard *St. Paul* in November 1899 he had cabled from 70 miles (110 kilometers) out in the Atlantic back to the Needles, located on the Isle of Wight's western tip. Those first sea bulletins were preserved and printed inside issue I, volume I of the *Transatlantic Times*, progenitor of countless shipboard publications to follow.

Then, in February 1902, Marconi crossed from Southampton to New York aboard the American Lines's *Philadelphia*. Her masts had been heightened to 150 feet (45 meters) for improved reception. He and his team received regular daily transmissions, all of them dispatched from Cornwall's Poldhu as it receded astern. S.S. *Philadelphia*'s wireless installation also necessitated construction of shipboard's first radio shack. Repeated sessions in the wheelhouse proved "disruptive" and removing loud wireless equipment from that command space was essential.

There was no escaping it—early wireless was noisy. The radio historian Paul Bock told me that all spark gaps of the period proved "sudden, violent, and disruptive, creating a sharp sound ranging from a small gap's *snap*, such as a spark plug in a car, to a louder *bang* produced by a wider gap. That same spark also liberated light and heat." Transmission racket was said to be audible a mile away from Poldhu, buttressing yet again the need for wireless transmitters' remote locations.

Philadelphia's pioneering radio shack was never soundproof either. Indeed, wherever early wireless equipment was located aboard ship, the clatter and cracking of spark gaps was endemic. Rather than distracting occupants of the bridge, now the noise disturbed occupants of nearby passenger cabins and, always, rows of deck chair aficionados.

The following year, a Morse transmission tapped from Marconi's station at Glace Bay, Nova Scotia, to Poldhu served as the first intelligible transatlantic message, not mindless repetition of a single letter but a fully comprehensible text. The time had come for Marconi to establish a transmitter on American soil. Among other things, the Italian was anxious to dispute the outrageous assertion that the American Wireless Telegraph & Telephone Company claimed to have patented America's entire ether!

Yet why Marconi erected his U.S. station atop Cape Cod's unstable, shifting dunes instead of Maine's rocky coast is mystifying. But the Massachusetts cape remained his unrelenting choice.

Marconi's initial venue, the county seat at Barnstable, proved too far inland; his second choice, Chatham's Highland Light, was rejected by the locals. So South Wellfleet, halfway along the cape's north-trending arm between Chatham's "elbow" and Provincetown's "hand," became his third and final Cape Cod selection. Marconi broke ground there in 1901.

Completion of both of these historic Marconi shore stations, one at South Wellfleet and its twin at Poldhu, required extraordinary diligence. Situated high on the dunes overlooking deserted beach and unobstructed sea, they seemed ideal locations. Yet however geographically apropos, Wellfleet particularly proved gravely susceptible to bad weather, desolate coastline syndrome at work again. First elements of his Cape Cod installation were completely destroyed by a winter storm and Marconi had to start construction all over again.

When completed, MCC (Marconi Cape Cod) was huge, incorporating two adjacent structures, a powerhouse and nearby transmitter house. As aboard *Titanic* to come, segregating noisy power production from the aurally vulnerable transmitting/receiving venue was mandatory. In the powerhouse, a 45-horsepower kerosene "engine generator" churned out 2,200 volts, which could then be ramped up to 22,000 volts, thanks to a Tesla (Marconi's embittered rival again) transformer. A windowless, aboveground cement tunnel housing electrical cables delivered power to the nearby transmitter house.

Yet it was less the buildings than the antenna rising above them that astonished. Harry Behenna, a young hand aboard the Cornish lugger *Prima Donna*, inbound to Mevagissey, spotted Poldhu's tower quartet atop the cliffs and asked his father, "Why is there a ship in the land?" Laid out in a giant square, 200 feet (60 meters) a side, four 210-foot-high latticed wooden towers looked more like factory chimneys than ships' masts, rising above substantial concrete bases. Guy wires supporting them were anchored to crossed timbers buried some 8 feet in the sand.

Connecting the 200-foot gaps separating the tops of that tower square was a strong horizontal cable, supporting element for Marconi's composite aerial. Two hundred separate copper antennas, fed up from the transmitter house inside a short wooden tower abutting the cement tunnel, had to be individually attached, 50 antennas per side, to insulated connectors spaced 4 feet apart along each of the four cables.

It was a monumental and dangerous job. Riggers rode via suspended trolleys along the cable, hauling up messenger lines knotted to each contributing antenna. Those men toiling high in Cape Cod winds were more than telegraph linemen; they became deft aerial riggers, securing every component strand of that copper network at dizzying height.

Suspended in place, two hundred wires assumed the shape of an inverted square cone, an almost fairy-tale assembly that, like those earlier St. John's antennas, swayed and danced in the wind. This was the giant disseminator that Marconi needed to loft, wirelessly, a presidential message and its royal response across more than 2,000 miles (3,220 kilometers) of intervening ocean to his identical installation in Cornwall.

Formal recognition of Marconi's triumph occurred on 19 January 1903, when President Theodore Roosevelt dispatched a message of state to King Edward VII. The presidential text concluded: "I extend on behalf of the American people most cordial greetings." From Sandringham, the monarch replied: "I thank you most sincerely for the message I have just received from you through Marconi's transatlantic wireless telegraphy." His Majesty included the inestimable product-placement bonus of the inventor's name.

Within days, Marconi's bare copper aerials became coated with green verdigris, only one of the corrosion problems instigated by the salt-tanged moisture of the exposed sites. Both the Wellfleet and Poldhu stations also suffered from the fragility of the dunes on which they were erected as encroaching breakers eroded their sea frontage.

In 1917, when America entered World War I, the government closed down Cape Cod's installation and, postwar, both the tower quartet and the buildings were abandoned. In truth, that elaborate installation had become almost immediately redundant. Transatlantic traffic would revert from wireless back to wire, profiting from the convenience, dependability, and clarity of undersea cable transmission. The first transatlantic connector had been laid by that freak giant of 1858 designed by Isambard Brunel, the S.S. *Great Eastern*. However unsuccessful as a passenger carrier, she proved an invaluable cable ship, first employed in 1866. Over the next eight years, the vessel was instrumental in laying five transatlantic cables. Though Marconi's wireless miracle was abandoned as a continental connector, it would remain an infallible means of linking ships.

Marconi's father died in 1904. It would doubtless have confounded him that, five years later, his tinkering son Guglielmo would share the Nobel Prize for physics with German wireless pioneer Karl Ferdinand Braun. He never met Marconi's wife either. On 16 March 1905, Marconi married the Honorable Beatrice O'Brien at London's St. George's Church in Hanover Square. The daughter of Edward Donough O'Brien, 14th Baron Inchiquin, she was a slightly eccentric young woman whose Irish roots doubtless pleased Marconi's mother. The bride christened her husband Marky and he taught her Morse.

She bore him four children in all, three daughters and a son. Degna was born in 1908 and Gioia in 1916; a third daughter lived only a few weeks. The boy, Giulio Giovanni, was delivered to Beatrice at the Villa Griffone on 21 May 1910. (The family property had, interestingly, been left by Marconi *père* to Guglielmo rather than to his older brother or stepbrother.) Marconi wanted his son born there so that he would enjoy Italian nationality. Typically, the babe's father was not present but somewhere at sea. News of the birth was cabled simply to MARCONI ATLANTIC, a joyous signal that would be forwarded on and on by relays of dutiful Marconi telegraphers until the newborn's father was successfully traced.

By 1912 almost every North Atlantic steamer had been equipped with wireless and Marconi operators were stationed aboard nearly a thousand of them, 410 of British registry. The Marconi International Marine Communication Company's largest rival was Slaby's German firm Telefunken, but Marconi's men comfortably outnumbered them. Call signs for Marconi-manned ships began with the letter M (for Marconi) followed by two arbitrary letters: *Titanic*'s, for example, would be MGY, *Olympic*'s MKC.

What was the profile of those applying for Marconi's arduous training? They were young British subjects who were adjudged bright, willing, and literate. Candidates also had to have acute, undamaged hearing. Later, during the Cold War, certain Swedish naval recruits, it was discovered, could not monitor ASDIC signals to detect Soviet submarines prowling the Gulf of Finland because their ears had been irreparably damaged by years of listening to rock 'n' roll.

Marconi telegraphers were first obliged to pass the standard civil service examination required of employees serving the British Post & Telegraph System. Thus armed, they worked ashore over landlines for several months before applying to become shipboard telegraphers at the Marconi company's Liverpool wireless telegraphy school.

Those accepted underwent six months' training as Marconi men, drilled in what the students christened "the tin shed." In that drafty structure, part of the Seaforth Barracks, incoming recruits refined their transmitting and receiving skills, starting with heavy manual typewriters with alphabetical keyboards, on which, over repetitious weeks, they worked up to a proficiency Morsing speed of twenty-five words per minute. Ancillary training sessions taught them how to troubleshoot and maintain their onboard equipment.

The trainees' task was not made easier by the proliferation of three separate and partially conflicting codes. The Europeans had developed Continental or International Morse. Fifteen of the International code's twenty-six letters differed from the Yankee originals, largely because the German language demanded variables that Morse's original choices had not included. The Continental system mandated dashes of three times rather than two times the length of a dot; hence, message duration was marginally extended. One accidental but fortuitous by-product of the expanded pauses was that they helped clarify transmissions obscured by atmospheric interference.

Then the U.S. Navy entered the lists with its own, hopelessly inadequate code; only three letters of the system duplicated Morse's original and only four the Continental's. This meant that navy telegraphers were blindsided by merchant ship traffic, rendering them embarrassingly—nay, *dangerously*—incommunicado. Officious, unnecessary, and incomprehensible to everyone else, the navy code was soon abandoned.

Marconi's trainee telegraphists, hunched over keys in the tin shed deciphering and tapping out practice dispatches to their fellows, still had to be proficient in two codes. Even though Continental Morse became transatlantic's gold standard, American coastal vessels stubbornly adhered to Morse's original. Incomprehensibly, U.S. naval telegraphists were never taught Continental Morse.

In spite of those communication shortfalls, the devices linking disparate vessels at sea had much in common with America's old-fashioned party line, an early telephonic expedient necessitated when many households shared a single wire. Barring obvious emergencies, subscribers patiently awaited their turn to reach the operator, often eavesdropping shamelessly on chattering neighbors. Wireless operated in identical fashion, every dispatch common knowledge; any telegrapher with a receiver, headphones, and a knowledge of Morse was privy to all traffic.

Their Liverpool training concluded, Marconi's men were licensed and issued uniforms. On their peaked caps, entwined foliage encircled a gold-lace M. Double-breasted blue uniforms, fitted with eight brass buttons, looked like officers' rig. Patently not officers, Marconi men were not regular crew either, occupying a novel limbo that defied shipboard stratification. They lived in rarefied country atop the vessel and worked to schedules of their own devising. Significantly, candid shipboard photographs invariably show them alone in the frame. While most crew snapshots were affable, grinning groups, telegraphers remained de facto loners, isolated from their shipmates.

Aboard large vessels two operators were assigned, a more experienced senior and a junior colleague. The top man was paid monthly wages of £10, £6 from Marconi and an additional £4 from White Star; his subordinate's monthly stipend was £4 from Marconi with a supplementary £2 from the company.

Titanic's senior telegrapher would be twenty-five-year-old John George Phillips, nicknamed Jack, a five-year Marconi veteran who had grown up in the village of Farncombe, near Godalming, the son of a draper. He was teamed with Harold S. Bride, age twenty-two, from Nunhead. The younger man had been qualified only briefly, previously assigned to *Haverford* and then *Lusitania*. The two agreed informally that Phillips would assume the first six-hour night shift, from 8 P.M. until 2 A.M., after which Bride would relieve him until 8 A.M. Daytime watches were arranged to suit both men's convenience.

The Marconi equipment installed aboard *Olympic* and *Titanic* was state of the art, the world's most powerful. Components had been crated and dispatched from Marconi's huge Chelmsford factory for installation at Belfast. They came with a familiar price: the more power, the more noise. The system's beating heart was an intrusive, 5-kilowatt motor generator. In operation—and that electrical rotor spun whenever the set was activated—it emitted a penetrating whine that, had it shared the same room as the operator, would have made it impossible to hear, let alone decipher, incoming transmissions. In smaller vessels with less powerful sets the radio shack could be contained within one all-inclusive space, but such was not the case aboard *Titanic*.

On prototype *Olympic*, the radio room had been located along the port side of Boat Deck, with a neighboring cabin for the operators. But the whine of the generator's motor proved so deafening that, for second-of-the-class *Titanic*, naval architect Thomas Andrews reshuffled his Boat Deck layout, moving the officers' smoking room forward along the deckhouse's starboard side. In its vacated footprint, after consultation with Marconi experts, he ordained three contiguous but separate athwartship spaces to house the wireless components and operators.

The portside space, named the silent room, housed the generator, its noise muffled from the central operations room. The heavily insulated party wall deadened that offending whine, rendering it inaudible in the adjacent receiving and transmitting room.

Around the walls of that central space was every radio shack appurtenance—desk, chairs, wall clock, brass-shaded lamps, telegraph key, pneumatic tubes to and from the purser's desk, and leads connected to *Titanic*'s four-strand aerial stretched between the vessel's fore- and aftermast, 204 feet (62 meters) above the waterline. Although the room also had a telephone line connected to the ship's switchboard, there was, curiously, no direct communication with the bridge, an omission that, post-*Titanic*, would be retroactively corrected aboard *Olympic* and *Britannic* with speaking tubes linking radio shack with bridge.

The room had no window but daylight was admitted through a leftover skylight that had illuminated the smoking room. That original skylight overlapped, perforce, into the third, starboardside room, the telegraphers' living quarters. It proved an annoyance, admitting unwelcome daylight that violated the preferred, cavelike darkness of an inside cabin, vital for men obliged to sleep at odd hours round-the-clock. Like most of *Titanic*'s occupants, passengers and crew alike, they had no attached bathroom but used officers' facilities down the passage.

Marconi's men were the Edwardian equivalent of today's computer geeks, privy to a new and, to everyone else, baffling technology. They, and only they, fully comprehended that incoming threnody of *dits* and *dahs*. Their telegraphed signals spanned the sea miles separating steamships' upper decks, a vital web linking formerly isolated commands. In 1904, White Star's *Cymric*, bound from Liverpool to Boston, rescued survivors from the burning freighter *St. Cuthbert*. This was the first instance of a wireless transmission bringing news of a live rescue at sea.

That was a classic case of wireless good, but other wireless behavior was often less positive. To start with, shipboard telegraphers remained parochially loyal to their respective employers; Marconi operators frequently disparaged or even ignored German operators. Symptomatic of both camps was what reactionary, post-*Titanic* journalists referred to as "wireless anarchy." Egocentric and sometimes arrogant behavior came with the job for one good reason: no one on board, from captain to boiler boy, shared their skills. Trading on that invulnerability, telegraphers sometimes exhibited a devil-may-care attitude. These cocky young men established their own behavioral standards. Scattered across the ocean, sans supervision, they buttressed their aloofness with a wealth of shared jargon, incomprehensible to the uninitiated.

Their closest chums were, paradoxically, far away, fellow "sparks" aboard other ships with whom they remained in almost constant communication. Late-night gossip was endemic. Not atypical is a surviving fragment from 1911, dispatched by one of *Lusitania*'s Marconi men (possibly Harold Bride?) to telegrapher Ernest Hill aboard Red Star Line's *Lapland*. "*What are you drinking tonight? We are drinking champagne*." Many of those idle exchanges were no more than adolescent foolishness; other traffic was sometimes uglier, dispatched, as Cunard officer James Bisset suggested, "often in a profane or insulting manner."

Years before cell phones, Marconi men were the first texters: OM or OB (old man or old boy) was a commonly transmitted preliminary, evoking the good-old-boy network of the tin shed. They employed a host of other time-saving shortcuts. STBI meant standby, GE and GN, respectively, "good evening" and "good night." Some abbreviations were culled from other languages: C signaled "yes." DE, doubtless pinched from the French, meant "from." N was "no," "you" became U, and R was "are." The word "message" was shortened to MSG, "traffic" to TFC. "Best regards" was conveyed enigmatically by the number 73, akin to later CB enthusiasts' 10–4. Later, when female operators were recruited, "love and kisses" was signified by 88. Disparagements had their own coded pejorative: LID branded an inept telegrapher as a "poor operator," QRL meant "keep quiet, I'm busy," and GTH a pithier "go to hell." The abrupt torrent GTHOMQRL said it all: "Go to hell, old man, I'm busy," A gentler sign-off might be TUOMGN: "Thank you, old man, good night."

Phillips and Bride oversaw the installation and activation of *Titanic*'s wireless at Belfast just prior to her sea trials. It was put to immediate use, dispatching trial results from Commodore Smith to Bruce Ismay in Liverpool. Their shipboard antenna was the same height, incidentally, as Marconi's great quadri-part antenna erected at South Wellfleet. Nighttime transmissions extended farther than those attempted by day, a phenomenon described as ionospheric propagation. Radio waves, disseminated from an antenna high in the air, travel flat; as they radiate horizontally from their source, the curvature of the earth falls away beneath them, curtailing distant reception. But after dark low-frequency waves in use at the time were refracted back toward earth, bouncing down, in effect, from what was called the ionosphere's D-level, hence extending farther across the globe's surface. Marconi, it was said, did not initially understand ionospheric propagation, mystified as to why his invention's performance improved so after dark. That evening, in between bouts of Liverpool traffic, Phillips and Bride indulged in every Marconi man's inevitable experimentation: how far at night? They raised Egypt's Port Said with ease, 3,000 miles (4,800 kilometers) from Belfast.

Titanic's inquiries desk, located on the starboard side of C Deck, was connected to the central operators' room by pneumatic tube. Passengers wishing to send a cable were given a telegraph form on which they spelled out their message, each word entered within its own printed box. Then an assistant purser folded it inside a brass cylinder, topped and tailed with a felt insulating collar of the same diameter as the brass tube into which he inserted it. Once a pneumatic charge had rocketed it four decks higher, the cylinder plopped into a wire basket on the radio room desk.

The duty telegrapher twisted it open, extracted the slip, recorded the sender's name, cabin number, and cable length into his *procés verbal* or logbook, computed the charges, and, together with any backlog of previously submitted forms, dispatched them into the ether.

A typical *Titanic* message to the States early in the crossing came from first class passenger William Sloper to his father in Hartford.

I am on the maiden voyage of the new S.S. Titanic arriving in New York Wednesday morning. Hope you will meet me and look her over. William

His father received it at exactly the same time as delivery of his *Hartford Courant*, headlined with news of the vessel's foundering.

Passengers were charged 12 shillings and sixpence for the first ten words, and ninepence a word thereafter. Sloper's twenty-seven-word message cost him 25 shillings and sixpence. Merely by employing what was already described as "cablese," the following eleven-word précis would have sufficed.

Arriving NYC aboard Titanic Wednesday A.M. see you on pier William

Half the fun of cables dispatched in extenso from a new ship in midocean was showing off. On the same day, equally affluent Richmond banker Robert Daniel advised his mother in West Virginia simply: "On board Titanic."

Though not cheap, cables represented only a modest investment for first class passengers. To shrink cables' length, steamship lines published an extensive list of word-saving abbreviations. For only fifty cents, Boston's *Adams Cable Codex* sold a collection of more than nine thousand sentences. "One code word," the editors promised, "covers sentences ranging from two to seventy words."

The simple but indicative word ANNOY signified "Departure postponed, will explain by letter." BUNG delivered more distressing news: "Baggage all left behind, cable instructions." Hamburg-America Line included in its code list the useful though grim eventuality EMBALO: "Embalmed the body, and shipped by steamer." In that same collection lurked an even bleaker abbreviation: RAPIDO for "Rapidly sinking." Obviously, for the system to be effective, recipients ashore needed a copy of the same code to decipher dispatches from their budget-minded, peripatetic correspondents.

Although the Marconi men's salaries were paid partially by White Star, that expense was more than offset by revenue from passenger and official ship traffic. However odd it might seem for companies to encourage coded abbreviations, the very existence of those shortcuts frequently encouraged passengers to send cables. And it was from the volume of traffic, rather than individual message lengths, that profits accrued.

The presence of wireless transmitters on board and ashore represented a revolutionary convenience. Nobody put it better than Marconi himself, who was staying in New York's Holland House when *Titanic* struck the iceberg. Reporters quizzing him moments after the tragedy were advised almost laconically, "That is one of the things that wireless is for. It has simply done what it was meant to do."

It did more after *Titanic*'s loss. An agreement was reached at that year's London Radio Conference, promulgating all maritime wireless stations to observe two radio silences each hour, during which operators might monitor airwaves for possible distress calls. This earliest convention was eventually standardized worldwide into two fixed periods, positioned at three minutes after every quarter to and three more after the quarter past. Listeners would tune in to what was designated the International Distress Frequency.

One aftermath of Marconi's *Titanic* linkage is intriguing. The wireless inventor and his family had been invited to sail on the maiden voyage of the latest White Star vessel. But urgent business in Manhattan required that Marconi arrive earlier than *Titanic*'s projected 18 April disembarkation. Marconi booked a cabin aboard faster *Lusitania*, sailing from Liverpool on 7 April. After taking care of his New York obligations, he planned on returning to England on the eastbound leg of *Titanic*'s maiden voyage.

Beatrice and the children, meanwhile, had accepted the original westbound invitation, despite Guglielmo's absence. But fate intervened: the infant Giulio, incapacitated by what the Edwardians described as "baby fever," was forbidden to travel.

So it was that Beatrice and four-year-old Degna, on the afternoon of 10 April, stood on the beach below the latest Marconi manse, Eaglehurst, an improbable eighteenth-century folly, ringed with flag-topped towers overlooking Southampton Water. Mother and daughter watched as the White Star giant steamed past without them, headed majestically for the Channel.

Had Marconi's son *not* been sick, had Beatrice and the children sailed as planned, there is every probability that, as first class passengers, they would have survived. But had Guglielmo been traveling with them, would he have been permitted to enter their lifeboat? If Colonel John Jacob Astor was denied permission to join his bride, Guglielmo Marconi might easily have suffered the same fate. That would have created one of history's remarkable ironies, that the inventor of the device that saved the lives of 703 survivors would not be among them.

With ship-to-ship wireless transmission a transatlantic commonplace by 1912, the stage is set for the April catastrophe that would engulf *Titanic*.

CHAPTER 2

GLITTERING NIGHT

[There were] whiskers round the lights.

Titanic quartermaster George Rowe

On a clear night, you can see a berg away off by its glitter. They glisten like an illuminated glass palace.

Donald Sutherland, *Parisian's* wireless operator

We are in the icebergs. The boat has a little hole in it downstairs. I think that to save a panic with the women, they are putting some of them off in lifeboats.

Titanic passenger Lucian Smith to his young wife, Mary Eloise

Icebergs combine awe and menace in paradoxical tandem. How bizarre that something so extraordinarily beautiful should be so lethal, the maritime equivalent of tropical blossoms that are poisonous.

Their abundance south of Cape Race that night of 14 April 1912 evoked the heightened reality of a Christmas card. Farther north in the Arctic, tide- or wind-driven icebergs are often in threatening motion; these were still. Everything was still. There was neither wind nor fog. Seas were unnaturally calm and the atmosphere crystal clear. There had been a spectacular sunset, which many *Titanic* passengers had viewed from already frigid open decks. Later, a vault of stars would gleam overhead, illumining that white/black seascape to perfection. Indeed, so bright were stars along the horizon that many mistook them for ships' lights. Seventeen-year-old passenger Jack Thayer remembered that they "appeared to stand right out of the sky, sparkling like cut diamonds."

More than one participant that night incorrectly recalled moonlight, but there was almost none. Although April 1912 was what was called a blue moon month, with full moons on the second and the thirtieth, during the night of the fourteenth only the faintest crescent of a waning moon adorned the eastern sky. That glittering night was almost solely illuminated by starlight, amplified by occasional flares of aurora borealis along the northern horizon.

No harbinger of maritime danger was apparent save for that forbidding iceberg array. Its presence was common knowledge, routinely reported by the masters of inbound steamers reaching New York. From the first of the year until April, the accumulation had grown ominously. In January, eight ice sightings were recorded and the figure doubled for February. March numbers receded to five but increased substantially the following month: during the first half of April alone, twenty-two arriving vessels testified to overwhelming ice presence.

Among the most detailed of those April reports came from the master and passengers of *Carmania*, which tied up in New York on 14 April. The Cunarder had negotiated a huge ice field by daylight on the afternoon of Thursday, 11 April.

Captain Daniel Dow (nicknamed "Fairweather Dow") recorded: "I have never seen field ice so far south." He counted at least twenty-five towering bergs, each of which he estimated to be 400 feet (120 meters) high, creating miniature mountain ranges stretching as far as the eye could see, imprisoned in ice. Though that field looked compacted, waves of a running sea sometimes set its apparently solid surface undulating. Suggested young passenger Claudia Sturm: "It was beautiful but it was mighty scary."

Working his way westward, Captain Dow was often stymied, momentarily finding no lead or opening through which to continue penetrating the pack. He also discovered that the ice field generated its own microclimate. At 1:35 P.M. on the eleventh, he was stopped by fog and had to proceed dead slow, sounding the ship's whistle repeatedly. Then, just after 3 P.M., the weather cleared and

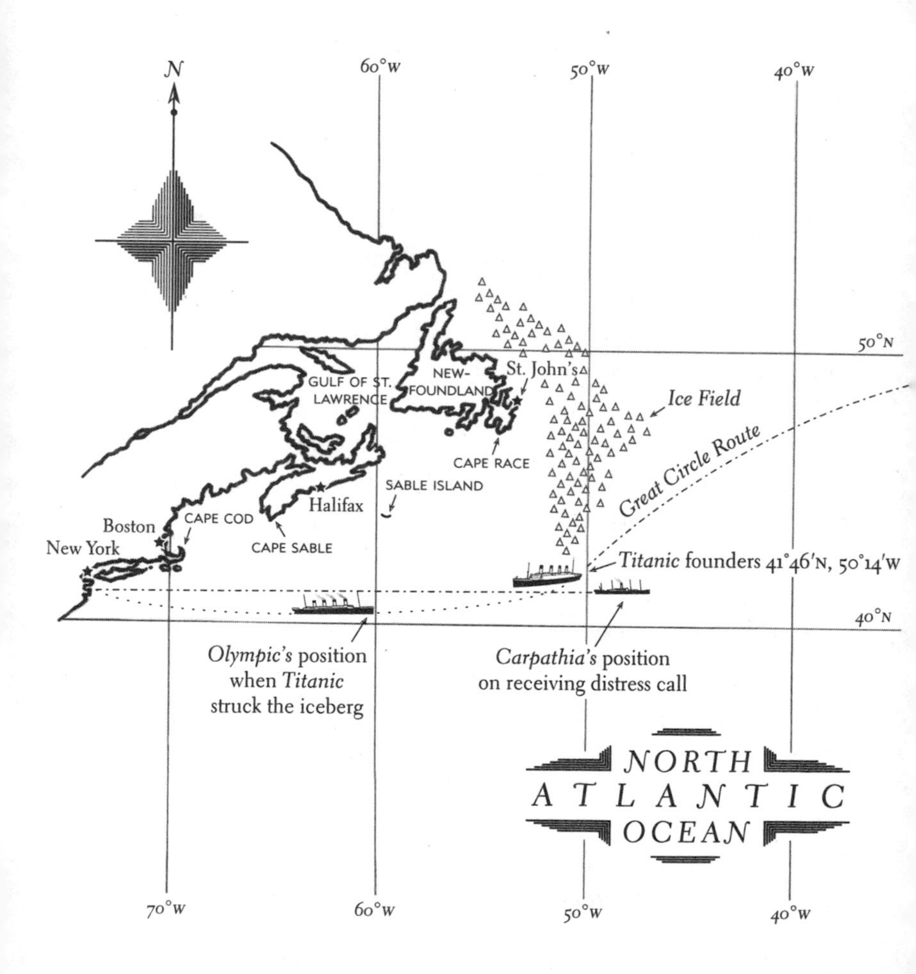

RMS *Titanic*'s Catastrophic Iceberg Encounter

2340 hours, 14 April 1912

he resumed full speed. An hour later, *Carmania* was again enveloped in dense fog, which after half an hour once again cleared miraculously.

Captain Dow and *Carmania* nearly became involved in a rescue when, from farther south, the French Line's *Niagara* broadcast a distress call, reporting that she had suffered damage to her hull and needed assistance. Dow started steaming *Carmania* toward her until a subsequent dispatch annulled the earlier request. He continued southward regardless, finally emerging from the ice and resuming course west to New York.

At first, it was thought that the profusion of ice obtruding so far south that April was part of a recurring eight-year phenomenon; similar conditions had been noted in 1896 and 1904. But other mariners insisted it was not cyclical, merely the aftereffects of a succession of ferocious March nor'easters that had agitated Labradorean waters, thrusting a welter of bergs, growlers, and field ice south into the North Atlantic shipping lanes. Aboard *Carpathia*, Captain Arthur Rostron told one of his officers, "Ice has come south very early this year. There must have been an early thaw on the Labrador Coast."

For almost every Atlantic liner, proximity to the ice of the far north was a given. Eastbound and westbound, masters adhered to the fast and economical great circle route connecting old world with new. After completion of that 1,634-nautical-mile (3,026 kilometers) arc from Ireland's Fastnet to longitude 47° W, latitude 41° 30′ N, westbound steamers had reached what was called in navigational bridge jargon "the corner." Arrival at the corner signaled both the end of the great circle and the fact that an additional 1,222 miles (2,263 kilometers) remained to New York. A new course would be established at that point: a starboard turn pointed the vessel's bows almost due west. After *Titanic* foundered, any cutting or shortchanging of the corner was prohibited.

From sea level, the ice field of April 1912 seemed endless, a blockade extending, some hazarded, for ten degrees of latitude, from 41° to 51° North and 3 degrees of longitude, from 49° to 52° West. Since one degree equals 60 nautical miles (111 kilometers), 10 signified 600 miles; 3 degrees comprised a longitudinal dimension of 180 nautical miles (333 kilometers). The worst of the field was estimated by bridge observers to be, overall, at least 30 by 15 nautical miles. But whatever its acreage, it remained a daunting hazard that lay waiting for imprudently driven *Titanic*.

Today's cruise ships are glazed with abandon, offering passenger unlimited observation through windows in every direction. But *Titanic*, more sparingly fenestrated against the inevitability of North Atlantic winter storms, offered only restricted panoramas from indoors. The best views were obtained through standard cabin portholes because the glass of too many suites and public rooms was obscured by decorative frippery, their often leaded glass panes sometimes framed with land-based casements. In first class's dining room, electric "sunlight" installed between interior casement and exterior porthole provided the comforting illusion of perpetual fair weather.

These touches were symptomatic of White Star's celebrated passenger indulgence. Thomas Ismay's company had achieved success by cosseting its largely American and often fragile clientele; gentleness and gentility were endemic aboard his vessels, as opposed to the hard-riding discomfort of admittedly faster Cunarders.

In fact, nobody aboard *Titanic* could take in the spectacle of that winter wonderland because the vessel was approaching rather than paralleling the ice field the way *Carmania* had. Few passengers saw the fatal iceberg slip past, although first class passenger Karl Behr, who walked forward to his fiancée's cabin, noted that ice "had gathered in the porthole" of her starboardside cabin after the impact.

Initial reaction to the collision was bemused disinterest. Those aroused by the impact exhibited scant curiosity, perhaps an understandable response from those booked aboard the world's biggest steamship; the larger the vessel, the greater its occupants' sense of impunity. An ice graze, it was felt, should not seriously affect a liner of *Titanic*'s pretension. Karl Behr might have spoken for all his fellow passengers: "To our minds, the idea of the *Titanic* sinking was preposterous." Several among the crew downgraded the impact to a thrown propeller blade.

Among the earliest realists were the vessel's five postal officers, two British and three American, none of whom survived. They were spotted by first class passengers Norman and Bertha Chambers. Norman had been reading in bed at the time of the collision and adjudged the impact "so slight as if we had run into a piece of timber," but he also recalled that there followed "a jangling as that of chains being dragged along the side of the ship."

Once dressed and out in the alleyway, Mr. and Mrs. Chambers encountered the postal staff, identified by armloads of damaged letters and the fact that their trousers "were wet up to the knees." Here was irrefutable, firsthand evidence of an E Deck inundation, but a passing steward neutralized the presumed urgency with the advice, "Everything is all right now, sir, you may turn in."

Just after midnight, second class passenger Edwina Troutt encountered a steward exhibiting similar indifference, busily polishing brass. When she marveled at his absorption in such a mundane task, he confided, "Oh, I 'ave been in these skirmishes before. I'm going to get me work done."

Back in first class, Victorine Chaudanson returned to her cabin for some warmer clothes, emerging from it only just in time to avoid being locked inside by her steward. It was orders, he apologized, to prevent jewelry thefts and also to retain more buoyancy by creation of additional enclosed compartments.

Also in first, Martha Stephenson and Elizabeth Eustis were sisters from Haverford, Pennsylvania. Earlier that evening, Martha had borrowed a book from the library about Shackleton's *Nimrod* expedition to Antarctica; as she admired the illustrations, it never occurred to her that she would ever see an iceberg herself.

The two women were of mixed emotions when the 11:40 impact woke them. Grabbing her bathrobe, Elizabeth went on deck to investigate. Martha stayed in the cabin, its open porthole chilling her to the bone. Bedroom steward John Penrose, who would not survive, assured her, "It's only cold, go back to bed. It's nothing at all."

What finally galvanized Martha into dressing was, curiously, the sight of some shoes. She had noticed that a man across the alleyway regularly put his shoes out for the ship's "boots" to polish each evening. But that night, after the collision, she saw him bring them hastily back inside. For some reason, their retrieval got her moving. When Elizabeth returned, they dressed carefully and warmly, as though getting ready for breakfast.

Elmer Taylor, a successful American inventor and manufacturer, was in his C Deck cabin. His wife, Juliet, was reading while toasting her feet before the electric fire. Resting his head on the pillow, Taylor noticed at 11:40 a "slight lift" of the vessel, followed shortly by the cessation of engine revolutions. He got dressed, lit a cigar, and, as he told Juliet, went on deck "to nose about and see if I can be of any assistance." He found a small chunk of ice on deck and, having first advised his wife about the iceberg, continued farther along C Deck to the cabin housing Fletcher Lambert-Williams, whose acquaintance he had made on the boat train. Fletcher lay in bed reading, smoking a cigar, and nursing a highball. "I've brought you some ice for your drink," joshed Taylor.

Such insouciance would not last. Over the succeeding hour, frissons of increasing alarm spread insidiously. For passengers aboard a stricken vessel, the hardest adjustment is crossing that knife edge separating complacency from concern. But unsettling evidence was accumulating. *Titanic* had undeniably stopped, billowing steam clouds were roaring from the first three funnels into the night, there was a perceptible list to starboard and then to port, davits had been swung out, and life-jacketed women and children were being hastened up staircases. As chilling as the night air greeting them outdoors on Boat Deck was the realization that their vessel was apparently in mortal danger.

Every ship in or near that ice field on the night of 14 April 1912 would achieve notoriety, seagoing flies imprisoned in saltwater amber. The happenstance of their presence would unite them forever, unwitting players in an epic maritime drama. By 1912 wireless was standard equipment aboard almost every vessel. The only ship near *Titanic* lacking wireless was Hamburg-America's *Deutschland*, not the company's famous 1900 record breaker but a disabled "tank steamer" or tanker. Periodically rendered incommunicado were smaller, Marconi equipped steamers whose lone telegraphers had to shut down transmitters so they could sleep.

Herewith a roll call of those incidental participants that sought to penetrate, bypass, or wait out that blockade of ice, an accidentally gathered flotilla of differing tonnage, nationality, and destination.

British vessels predominated. Foremost, as far as *Titanic* was concerned, was consort *Olympic*. She had arrived in New York on 10 April and then departed for Southampton on the thirteenth at three o'clock in the afternoon. When *Titanic* struck the iceberg at 11:40 P.M. the following night, *Olympic* was at 40.52° N, 61.18° W, sailing eastward for the corner but still 505 miles distant.

Other White Star players included smaller *Baltic*, which, proceeding to Liverpool, immediately turned back on hearing *Titanic*'s distress call. Her fleetmate *Celtic* was headed in the opposite direction to New York.

Three Cunarders were among the dramatis personae—*Caronia* crossing eastbound to Liverpool and *Franconia* steaming westbound for New York. *Carpathia* had departed New York three days earlier, carrying a group of Americans on a spring cruise to the Mediterranean. Atlantic Line's *Minnewaska* trod the fringes of the stage, having sailed from New York on 15 April. Atlantic Transport Line's *Mesaba* was steaming west for New York.

Six German vessels had walk-on parts. North German Lloyd's *Prinz Friedrich Wilhelm* was proceeding from Hoboken to Plymouth. *Frankfurt*, also sailing east, estimated that she was only 24 miles from *Titanic* at the time of the sinking. Hamburg-America's participants—in addition to tanker *Deutschland*—included *Blucher*, *Amerika*, and *Ypiranga*.

Representing the French Line were *La Touraine*, crossing to France, and *La Bretagne*, headed in the opposite direction for New York. Westbound *Noordam* was the only Dutch merchantman present. Two Canadian Pacific vessels, westbound *Mount Temple* and *Empress of Britain*, first of the entire *Empress* class, were also within wireless range. *Mount Temple* had departed Antwerp on 3 April, destination New York. *Birma*, the ex–*Arundel Castle* liner sailing now for the Russian American Line, was headed from New York to its home port of Libau.

The Allan Line's *Parisian* was en route to Philadelphia with an intermediate call at Halifax while the same company's *Virginian* sailed eastbound, from Halifax to Liverpool. Crossing westbound from London to Boston without passengers but with a load of timber was the Leyland Line's *Californian*.

Of those random players four would assume major roles: *Titanic*, of course; her approaching sister ship *Olympic*; Cunard's rescue ship *Carpathia*, immortalized forever, and, for very different reasons, *Californian*. Her master, Captain Stanley Lord, would spend the rest of his life trying vainly to escape worldwide censure for his failure to assist nearby *Titanic*.

A fifth, Canadian Pacific's *Mount Temple*, commanded by Captain James Moore, has become another reluctant performer, as reports have emerged of dissension between the master and his officers as well as several passengers. One stated that at two o'clock on the morning of the fifteenth, just as *Titanic* was sighted, *Mount Temple's* deck lights were suddenly extinguished and her engines stopped. Another testified that Captain Moore "hove to his ship in spite of the entreaties of his officers that he rush to the aid of *Titanic.*"

Parisian and *Virginian* would become quasi-featured players, erroneously identified as having participated in the rescue. Many increasingly desperate New Yorkers assumed that, because of the two Allan Line vessels' *Titanic* proximity, they might have embarked survivors. It was untrue, alas, but for several days, until inbound *Carpathia* set the record straight, families hoped that additional survivors might have been rescued by either one. An inescapably sad fact was that *Carpathia* alone picked up survivors; no other ship did.

Tunisian, another Allan Line fleetmate, would arrive in Liverpool on 17 April. Long before the iceberg encounter she had passed *Titanic* and signaled good luck. Harold Bride's laconic acknowledgment was "Many thanks good-bye."

Our frozen stage is set, our players poised. Though most of that inadvertent fleet played only minor parts, a précis of their cumulative dispatches re-creates that glittering night's wireless scenario, by turns intriguing, poignant, heartbreaking, and ultimately grim. The span of that wireless fusillade was *Titanic*'s collision with the iceberg at 11:40 P.M. Sunday night, 14 April, and her foundering two hours and forty minutes later, at 2:20 A.M., Monday, 15 April.

Preliminary exchanges started first thing Sunday morning at nine when *Caronia* alerted oncoming *Titanic*: "Bergs, growlers, and field ice in 42 degrees North from 49 to 51 West. at 1:42 P.M." This was the first of six ice warnings *Titanic* received.

Amerika was next at 11:20 that same morning. In a message addressed to *Titanic* and forwarded to Washington's Hydrographic Office and Cape Race, telegrapher Otto Reuter warned that *Amerika* had passed two icebergs "at 41° 27′ North and 50° 8′ West." For years, Reuter agonized that his message had been either ignored or received too late. *Titanic*'s latitude at the time of the collision was 41° 46′ N and (corrected) longitude 50° 14′ W. The variation with Reuter's observed bergs was nearly 20 sea miles (37 kilometers) to the north and an additional 6 sea miles (11 kilometers) east. Reuter was not alone in claiming to have pinpointed the actual iceberg that might sink or had sunk the White Star vessel. More than one survivor as well as numerous *Carpathia* passengers and crew claimed to have spotted *Titanic*'s frozen nemesis, an almost impossible task, given the profusion of drifting bergs the length of the ice field's margin.

Five minutes later, at 11:40, *Noordam* chimed in with a third alert: "Much ice." Then eastbound *Baltic* joined the chorus, filling in more detail for fleetmate *Titanic*: "Icebergs and large quantities of field ice in 41° North to 51° North, 49° to 52° West. Wish you and Titanic all success." Theirs was the fourth warning, concluding with a pro forma maiden voyage sign-off between fellow company telegraphers.

There was, horrifying to relate, a crippling shutdown of *Titanic*'s wireless for much of the afternoon and early evening of that Sunday. However powerful or expensive, *Titanic*'s Marconi equipment was not trouble free. Shortly after noon, a wire somewhere in the transmitter had escaped its insulation and was shorting out against its iron housing, abrogating all incoming or outgoing transmissions. Over that afternoon and early evening, Phillips and Bride spent seven hours patiently disassembling the transmitter, searching for and finally correcting the rogue element. Neither slept all afternoon.

"For want of a horse . . ." Had they not succeeded, had *Titanic*'s wireless capability been compromised during the hours that followed, transatlantic history would have been unbearably altered.

Not until 12:15 A.M. the following morning, thirty-five minutes after the collision, did Captain Smith order Phillips to broadcast the first distress call. A CQD went out (Phillips never resorted to the updated SOS) with an incorrect longitudinal reading of 50° 24′ West for the ship's position, amended moments later to 50° 14′ West by relieving officer of the watch Joseph Boxhall.

Frankfurt and *La Touraine* were first receptors. Given the position, they responded only "OK, standby." Dispatches headed CQD inspired brevity.

Captain Stulpin of nearby *Birma* somehow jumped the gun. In his official report submitted to company headquarters, he testified that Phillips's CQD was logged in to his wireless shack at 11:45, five minutes after the collision. But since his report included the corrected longitudinal figure, it must have been written with inaccurate hindsight. Perhaps *Birma* employed a different time system or perhaps the man translating Russian into English erred. In any event, only a hundred miles distant, Stulpin mustered an additional shift of stokers, changed course, and pressed toward *Titanic*.

Carpathia somehow missed Phillips's first distress call because at 0025, ten minutes after it was dispatched, her operator Harold Cottam asked Phillips on *Titanic* if he realized that "MCC [Marconi Cape Cod] was sending a batch of messages for you."

Wasting no time, Phillips responded brusquely.

"Come at once. We have struck a berg. It's a CQD OM [a distress situation, old man]. Position 41.46 N. 50.14 W."

All business, Cottam tapped back: "Shall I tell my captain? Do you require assistance?"

"Yes, come quick," was Phillips's immediate response.

From their first exchange, perhaps divine prescience, Cottam and Phillips remained calm, expedient, and to the point, establishing an enviable wireless relationship. In his report later submitted to Cunard's head office, written aboard *Carpathia* the day after his arrival in New York, Rostron establishes the hour of 12:34 on the morning of the fifteenth as his first exposure to Cottam's alert. In the same report, curiously, Rostron makes more than one reference to *California*, dropping its terminal *n*, a common press error but surprising from an involved Cunard master.

The next moment we get a flavor of the difficulties under which Phillips worked, from his dispatch to *Ypiranga*.

"CQD here [is my] corrected position 41.46 N. 50.14 W. Require immediate assistance. We have collision with iceberg. Sinking. Can hear nothing for noise of steam." Safety valves on all three of *Titanic*'s working funnels had been tripped to forestall boiler explosions. Up on Boat Deck the racket was deafening.

Californian's only *Titanic* feeler was a fiasco. Earlier that night, at 11:00 P.M., well before the collision, operator Cyril Evans had tapped out informatively to Phillips: "We are stopped and surrounded by ice."

Even today, Phillips's response jars.

"Shut up, shut up, you are jamming my signal. I am working Cape Race."

It remained the first and only exchange between those two starring players. An hour later, after the collision but before *Titanic*'s first distress call, Evans was drifting off to sleep, having told *Californian*'s amateur wireless enthusiast, the ship's third officer Charles Groves, that it was all right for him to listen in on *Californian*'s set, which would prove temporarily inoperable.

At 12:30, after receiving *Titanic*'s CQD, *Mount Temple* answers: "Our captain reverses ship. We are about 50 miles off."

Four minutes later, Phillips exchanged an urgent barrage with John Durrant, *Frankfurt*'s Marconi operator.

"Are you coming to our assistance?"

"What is the matter with you?" Durrant Morsed back.

"We have struck an iceberg and sinking. Please tell captain to come."

"OK. Will tell the bridge right away."

"OK, yes, quick."

At 12:45, Phillips tried raising *Olympic*. His opposite number, hunched over the key of *Olympic*'s equally powerful set, was senior telegrapher Ernest Moore. In a later summation of that night's events, *Olympic*'s Captain Herbert James Haddock would submit a glowing testimonial to Marconi headquarters, recommending promotion for "thoughtful, reliable" Moore. Despite that accolade, in retrospect, the man's comprehension of Phillips's desperation borders on the obtuse.

Fifteen minutes passed before Phillips could arouse any response. When contact was finally established, it initiated a dreamlike exchange between the two White Star operators. At 1 A.M. Phillips tapped to Moore: "We have struck an iceberg." There was no reply.

Ten minutes later, Phillips followed up with an amplified bulletin: "We are in collision with berg. Sinking head down 41°46′ N 50°14′ W come soon as possible."

An instant later, Phillips sent yet a third plea: "Captain says get your boats ready. What is your position?"

At last, *Olympic* responds with her position and inquires: "Are you steering southerly to meet us?"

Counters Phillips: "We are putting the women off in boats." That almost identical message would be sent three times over the next five minutes, the last with the addenda: "Can not last much longer."

Still the penny does not drop. After a further five-minute pause, *Olympic* inquires: "What weather did you have?" Not what weather *do* you have, but *did* you have, as though Moore wanted to clarify how or why the collision had occurred. "Clear and calm," explained Phillips, suiting the import of his message. Finally, nearly an hour after first contact, Moore signaled: "Am lighting up all boilers as fast as can."

However heartening, Captain Haddock's hoped-for intervention was essentially fruitless. Traveling at top speed of over 22 knots, *Olympic* would be unable to reach her stricken sister for twenty-four hours. As it was, *Olympic*'s final deployment was parking immobile for most of Tuesday, 16 April, relaying to both shores lists of survivors' names Morsed from *Carpathia*. The next day, Haddock was ordered by Liverpool to resume passage for Southampton. Only then were her stunned passengers allowed to send their own wireless dispatches.

Then Cape Race passed along to *Virginian* a hopelessly inaccurate assessment. Obviously, that shore-based Marconi operator had missed *Titanic*'s first exchange with *Carpathia*, along with much of that night's traffic.

"Please tell your captain this: the Olympic is making all speed for Titanic, but his [Olympic's] position is 40.32 N. 61.18 W. You are much nearer to Titanic. The Titanic is already putting women off in the boats, and he says the weather there is calm and clear. The Olympic is the only ship we have heard say, 'Going to the assistance of the Titanic.' The others must be a long way from the Titanic."

Not so. At 12:30 A.M. *Mount Temple* had advised Phillips: "Our captain reverses ship. We are about 50 miles off." Three quarters of an hour later White Star's *Baltic* signaled to Caronia: "Please tell Titanic that we are making towards her." *Caronia* did, relaying on to Phillips: "Baltic coming to your assistance." Only moments later, *Baltic* reiterates: "We are rushing to you."

One nearby vessel seemed to pontificate. Phillips advised *Asian* of *Titanic*'s bleak situation just after one in the morning. Given *Titanic*'s coordinates, when the operator reported it to the bridge, *Asian*'s captain asks for verification of the position.

At quarter to two, Cottam could just decipher a last despairing call from Phillips. "Come as quickly as possible old man: the engine room is filling up to the boilers." Then *Titanic*'s signal faded. Phillips could no longer transmit.

Ten minutes later Cape Race reported to *Virginian*: "We have not heard from Titanic for about half an hour. His power may be gone."

Not quite. *Frankfurt*, 172 miles distant, called *Titanic*, inquiring innocently: "What is the matter with U?" Phillips, increasingly fraught, has sufficient power for a brief riposte, overheard by *Caronia*: "You fool STBI [standby] and keep out."

At 02:17, three minutes before *Titanic* foundered, *Virginian* suggested that her operators switch to the emergency set. There was no response. At that moment, *Titanic*'s lights were dimming to an orange glow as the hull's after half reared skyward, poised for the final plunge.

The exchange of ice reports, location information, and assurances of rescue and relief petered out, the former flurry reduced to spasmodic, wistful feelers. Three minutes later *Virginian* queries *Olympic*: "Have you heard anything about Titanic?" *Olympic* responds in the negative but suggests she is keeping strict watch.

At 8:45 the following morning, *Olympic* telegrapher Moore would send a message via Sable Island to White Star's New York office: "Have not communicated with Titanic since midnight." (Another inaccuracy: the contorted Phillips/Moore exchange had started an hour *after* midnight.) Monitoring the night's latest developments, *Mount Temple*'s operator picks up Cottam aboard *Carpathia* Morsing *Titanic*, fifteen minutes after she has gone to the bottom: "If you are there we are firing rockets." Every twenty minutes, throughout his vessel's frantic race toward *Titanic*, Cottam continually tried arousing some response from the now sunk vessel.

He was not alone. Every telegrapher within that frozen arena clutched at straws. Just before 3:00 A.M., the Telefunken operator aboard *Birma* thought he heard a signal from *Titanic* and immediately dispatched a comforting if hopeless response: "Steaming full speed for you. Shall arrive you 6–0 in morning. Hope you are safe. We are only 50 miles now."

In fact, *Birma* would see *Carpathia* across an impassable expanse of the ice field. Stulpin, *Birma*'s master, had his operator find out if there were anything he could do; "Stand by" was Cottam's only response. The two ships, each steaming in the opposite direction, would try communicating just after noon on the fifteenth. After Stulpin dispatched a second query, he recorded: "We received the answer 'Shut up,' as our wireless installation was of a different system from Marconi."

Realism finally intruded aboard *La Provence*. Her operator dispatched a bleak signal to White Star's *Celtic* at 3:28: "Nobody has heard the Titanic for about 2 hours."

Just over an hour later *Birma* observed only: "We are 30 miles sw of Titanic."

When the sun came up on the morning of Monday the fifteenth all focus shifted to *Carpathia*. By 6:40 A.M., *Parisian* had overheard that the Cunarder already had some survivors aboard. An hour later, *Mount Temple* picked up another *Carpathia* report, saying that she had twenty boatloads of *Titanic* people accounted for.

After 8:00 *Baltic*, still diverted from her original eastbound heading and steaming for the position where *Carpathia* was taking on survivors, offered to share the load: "Can I be of any assistance to you as regards taking some of the passengers from you? Will be in position about 4:30. Let me know if you alter your position."

Cottam was instructed to reject the offer. Once the little White Star vessel *Baltic* was rebuffed, she headed at top speed for Liverpool, making up for lost time during her fruitless 134-mile westward detour.

Just before 9:00 A.M. Cottam suggested that two other nearby vessels resume course, clearly command relays originating from Rostron. The Cunard master had already instructed Captain Lord of the *Californian* to search for more survivors before conducting a brief memorial service over the spot. Now back on the bridge and all business, he advised *Baltic*: "Am proceeding to Halifax or New

York full speed. You had better proceed to Liverpool. Have about 800 *passengers* on board." His recommendation was redundant: *Baltic* had turned back forty-five minutes earlier.

Moments afterward, a similar message was dispatched to *Virginian*: "We are leaving here with all on board about 800 passengers. Please return to your northern course."

It was Rostron's second use of that obviously rough estimate of 800 survivors. In fact, there were 703 alive; four had died after coming aboard. Packed with essentially a doubled passenger load, *Carpathia* turned back to the west. Rostron had originally planned a closer landfall at Halifax but changed his mind after realizing that his *Titanic* survivors should be faced with as little intervening ice as possible.

Thus the crackling Marconi network, so recently fraught with urgent activity, fell silent as the supporting players dispersed. Life aboard every one of them would revert to normal, though it is safe to say that following the cataclysmic night of 14 April 1912, nothing in those bustling sea-lanes would ever be quite the same again.

CHAPTER 3

HORNBLOW AT QUEEN'S ISLAND

Pirrie has just persuaded me to order a ship and I don't know what the deuce I'll do with it.

Liverpool shipowner

The Titanic *is now about complete and will, I think, do the old firm credit tomorrow when we sail.*

Letter extract from Thomas Andrews to his wife, 9 April 1912

Ladies, you must get in at once. There is not a minute to lose. You cannot pick and choose your boat. Don't hesitate, get in! Get in!

Thomas Andrews on *Titanic*'s Boat Deck, 1:30 A.M., 15 April 1912

Poor Mr. Andrews came along, I saw in his face all I wanted to know.

Mary Sloan, *Titanic* stewardess

Brand-new Titanic *was no more. Now we must learn details of* the time when the vessel was even newer, about her design, construction, and launch at the gritty venue where she and prototype *Olympic* had been wrought. Belfast's Harland and Wolff was Europe's largest and most profitable shipyard. At the famous Queen's Island works, Viscount William Pirrie, guiding genius of the entire enterprise, together with his nephew by marriage, naval architect Thomas Andrews, had built and delivered both *Olympic* of 1911 and *Titanic* a year later. The yard's reputation for launching luxurious, groundbreaking tonnage was renowned throughout the maritime world.

It was 5 A.M., before daylight of a wet Belfast morning in November 1911. Despite the hour, men wearing caps, weatherproofs, and hobnail boots, with lunch pails swinging from their arms, tramped along the sleeping city's rain-swept streets in growing numbers. Their daily commute started with a brisk forty-minute walk. Frequently, multiple occupants left houses by the same gate, fathers who had started their working lives as apprentices accompanied now by sons following in parental footsteps. All were bound for the site of the city's largest employer, Harland and Wolff.

One such trio that raw day was George Wade, a skilled joiner, and his two sons, aged fourteen and sixteen, who had been indentured at the shipyard as apprentices just as he had. The privilege had cost their father a £5 investment for each lad, money that would be refunded only when and if each successfully completed his six-year apprenticeship.

At a pier entrance, the men deposited ha'penny fares, leaving the glistening cobbles for the black iron decks of a waiting ferry. Old hands in the know stayed at the after end; those near the bow risked a dousing from the wake of a late Liverpool boat passing in a hurry.

A hundred-yard crossing delivered them across inshore waters of Belfast Lough onto Queen's Island. As the vessel nosed into the terminus, barriers clattered open and hundreds disembarked across a tilting pontoon to surge through the yard gates. Before them rose workshops, slipways, pump houses, and gantries, a huge industrial sprawl. Miami's Dodge Island is made from spoil dredged to create Government Cut; so too in Belfast Lough, as accumulated spoil dredged from the river Lagan made up the length of Queen's Island. Its two-and-a-half-mile central Queen's Road was, at the time, the longest stretch of straight municipal road anywhere in the kingdom.

The workers' haste was understandable, for they had already heard the shriek of the yard's steam whistle, a bronze triple-chime relic from a demolished ship mounted atop the power plant's roof. That imperious summons, called hornblow, echoed all over Belfast. The men had to punch the company's time clock by 6:00 A.M. before hastening to the various workshops.

They deposited their outer clothing and lunch pails, or "pieces," inside lockers, donned overalls, and started work for exactly two hours and twenty minutes. At precisely 8:20 A.M., there was a forty-minute break for breakfast before a second return to work at nine.

Another forty-minute break—identified, overgenerously, as "the meal hour"—would follow at 1:00 P.M. for lunch. Four hours later the working day was over.

The two younger Wades were assigned elementary tasks in the dust of the timber shop, grading, sorting, cutting, and planing lengths of mahogany, walnut, sycamore and oak. Wade *père*, carrying his piece with him, spent his entire day aboard one of the great ships being fitted out, Harland and Wolff hull no. 401. He was one of dozens of joiners toiling on the graceful fantail shape and railing of the main staircase.

Once the men had clocked out their reverse commute began, another ferry ride ashore through early winter twilight and another forty-minute, largely uphill trudge home for tea, newspapers, and wives.

Harland and Wolff's name came from the yard's original owning partners, Edward James Harland and longtime UK resident but originally German Gustav Wilhelm Wolff, whose uncle Gustavas Schwabe was a Hamburg shipowner and investor. After founding the yard in 1860, the new partners' first vessel was the 1,500-ton sailing steamer *Venetian* for the Bibby Line. With four rakish masts and a single funnel, she was not dissimilar in profile to White Star Line's first steamer *Oceanic*, launched ten years later for the company's founder, Thomas Ismay. Both Ismays, Thomas and his son Bruce, who would become White Star's managing director after the turn of the century, enjoyed a close and congenial relationship with the Belfast yard.

Oceanic was the first of eighty-eight ships that the yard built for White Star. Only one of the company's fleet was not launched from the Belfast builders, a 102-foot wooden baggage tender called *Traffic*, delivered from Cheshire's Speakman, Runcorn yard in 1896. A second White Star tender, also called *Traffic*, would later service company vessels calling at Cherbourg.

With a larger output than rival John Brown's Scottish Clydeside establishment, Harland and Wolff was Britain's foremost shipyard. The Belfast yard was heavily involved with both White Star and Hamburg-America Line tonnage; the Scots were more likely to launch Cunarders.

Early in his tenure, Edward Harland had been confronted with the threat of a strike by workers hoping to organize a union. His response was abrupt: he fired the entire workforce and began hiring replacements. Not surprisingly, the organizers backed down in the wake of that iron-fisted rebuke. And it was doubtless Harland's ruthless response that set the tone for the company's unremitting stance toward its employees forever. Civilized bargaining between capital and labor would not happen for years; working conditions at the yard remained archaic, almost feudal, with management in tyrannical control. That same antilabor regime would continue under successive managements, including that of Canadian-born William James Pirrie, who arrived in Ireland at the age of two.

His grandfather James had been instrumental in the development of the city of Belfast. As a member of the Harbour Commission, Captain James Pirrie had spent thirty years seeing to the excavation, channeling, and maintenance of the originally contorted river Lagan. Despite the fact that James Pirrie was a familial name of clout and distinction in the city, his grandson William would start from the bottom at the shipyard, signing on as one of the premium or gentleman apprentices. The sponsor's fee for gentleman apprenticeships was 100 guineas rather than 5 pounds. But gentleman or no, Pirrie would make the same daily commute on foot as thousands of his future employees. From such lowly beginnings he would finally succeed Harland, after the director died in 1895. In July 1906, he would be elevated to the peerage, becoming Viscount Pirrie.

Pirrie's nephew by marriage Thomas Andrews chose the same route, another gentleman candidate. His first day at the yard took place on 1 May 1889, when he was just sixteen, beginning an apprenticeship that would last five years. The young man was pushed hard, assigned first to the joiners shop, then to the cabinet makers, and then on to a bewilderment of steel hulls rising on the ways. He was transferred to the main store, followed by stints in the shipwrights, patternmakers, and fitters shops. But of all the departments to which Andrews was assigned it was the drawing office where he excelled, exhibiting a talent that would direct him firmly into the demanding specialty of ship design. Small wonder for a boy whose fondness for ships at an early age had earned him the nickname "Admiral." His outstanding performance in the drafting and design shop guaranteed him the starting post of junior naval architect.

There was an additional fortuitous perk for the recent gentleman apprentice. Thanks to a judicious £5,000 investment contributed by his mother, the novice draftsman was rewarded with a small, part ownership of the yard and so would serve as both Harland and Wolff employee and employer.

Andrews was appointed chief designer in 1903. Had he lived, it would have been interesting to see if he made it to Harland and Wolff's helm. Pirrie succumbed to prostate cancer in 1924, when Andrews would have just been fifty-one. Clearly, the young naval architect's executive posture and style of management would have been different. Whereas Pirrie, in the manner of Harland before him, was a stubborn autocrat, Andrews flew a very different jib: sunny, appealing, and accommodating, he was universally popular on every level at Harland and Wolff, a gentleman in the true sense of the word.

Perhaps it is ruthlessness, however, that spells success in a shipyard's demanding top job. Andrews might well have proved too accommodating or understanding, lacking the adamantine edge that made things happen. Sadly, of course, details of his post-1912 performance remain forever unknown; that promising life ended off Cape Race at the age of thirty-nine.

Andrews's good nature was not restricted to Belfast but spread throughout White Star's fleet as he sailed aboard Harland and Wolff's newbuildings. One venerable North Atlantic truism posits an appalling gulf separating occupants of a company's ships at sea from supervisory personnel assigned to head office. Though many of the men behind those desks had started their company careers as crewmen at sea, once they swallowed the anchor, as it was called, they lost shipboard geniality, replacing earlier cooperation with a somehow aggrieved confrontation.

Thomas Andrews was one of the few who transcended that norm. Though never permanently assigned to duty at sea, he spent much time gauging the performance of his designs under way, anxious to determine how his drawing board output satisfied operational demands.

For most lower deck crewmen, naval architects are remote figures with whom they enjoy scant contact. But Andrews proved a refreshing exception, making it his business to inspect diligently every on-deck and 'tween-deck cranny. His attention to the minutest details was legendary, a preoccupation not confined to steel and teak. Andrews always chatted with many of the vessel's working inhabitants, not only bridge officers, engineers, and bosuns but humbler personnel as well, picking their brains for feedback. He recorded everything—whether compliment or complaint—in an ever-present notebook. Such was his receptive ear that crewmen often passed along sensible ideas as to how Andrews might improve their living conditions and quarters.

One perfect case in point was the apt suggestion made by an assertive young Irish stewardess assigned to a first class section aboard new *Olympic*. Violet Jessop was not shy about approaching Andrews shortly after he embarked for the vessel's maiden voyage in June 1911. For second of the class *Titanic*, at that moment being fitted out, Jessop respectfully proposed a refinement to the stewards' quarters. What they needed, she pointed out, were improved sanitary facilities. Thanks to her impetus and Andrews's clout they would be implemented aboard the new ship.

Violet never forgot him. When, on the maiden voyage, Andrews visited *Titanic*'s glory hole, shipboard nickname for stewards' quarters, by way of gratitude she and her shipmates presented him with a surprise gift, a smart polished cane to help offset the pain of troublesome varicose veins, a legacy of tramping the steel decks of so many new ships. Though delighted with his present Violet noted that he seemed tired and down on day three of his last voyage. He was longing for return to his family back in Belfast. Both his father and his wife were unwell and he was sad to be sailing westbound every day, "getting further from home," as he put it to Violet.

His ascendancy at the yard had coincided with a surge of ambitious newbuildings that were substantially enriched by his involvement. By the turn of the century the Queen's Island works boasted sufficient acreage to construct fourteen ships at the same time. In 1909 the yard's two largest launchways were slips no. 2 and no. 3, melded from an original trio. They lay side by side beneath Glaswegian Sir William Arrol's adjacent gantries, 840 feet by 270 feet (254 × 82 meters), erected above and covering each slipway. In simplest terms, those two elevated structures were essentially girdered roofs spanning the length and width of the berths, equipped with all manner of conveniences and assists for large-scale ship construction.

Those unprecedented slips had been specifically ordained for building what can only be described as megahulls no. 400 and no. 401. The first, christened *Olympic*, was already in service on the North Atlantic run to New York. The second, *Titanic*, was being fitted out for delivery to White Star in April 1912. Displacing in excess of 45,000 tons each, they were the two largest steamships in the world.

Atop each gantry stood a cantilevered crane capable of a three-ton lift with an outreach of 135 feet (40 meters). There were also three overhead travelers with a pair of ten-ton trucks on each, and five side-walking cranes spanning each berth. Vertical access for workers was improved by two separate elevator systems as well as an inclined roadway for wheeled delivery to every deck.

The same overhead framework also provided suspension for heavyweight construction paraphernalia, not only overhead cranes that could lower steel plates into position but also the giant lobster claws of hydraulic riveters that would attach many of them together. The movable jaws of those claws were cast of rigid steel; once correctly positioned, they ensured immediate and efficient closure. Instead of rivets being battered by two-man teams—backer-upper and human riveter—a jolt of compressed air completed the task.

The secret was a vigorous hydraulic expansion mechanism incorporated between the top claw elements, connected by reinforced hose to electrical compressors. The moment it was activated, with one pervasive hiss, those upper jaw elements were thrust apart. At the same instant, the casting's giant scissors' action squeezed the lower jaws convulsively together, instantly crushing the red hot rivet's protruding shank into a simulacrum rounded head.

Although the device had been used horizontally for the double bottoms, the curve of the bilges and plating up as far as D Deck required hand riveting. But from D Deck up to strength or B Deck, hydraulic riveting returned with a vengeance, the claws now deployed vertically. To diminish the frequency of butts and overlaps, Andrews had ordained oversize hull plates, the longest steel 36 feet (11 meters) by 6 feet (1.8 meters), weighing in at some 4 tons apiece.

The long plates' height of 6 feet had been selected to conform successfully to the reach of the hydraulic riveter's jaws. Slightly more than 6 feet separated terminal crushing ends from central hinge. That became the factor governing the optimum height of both vessels' upper strakes or plates. Once each plate had been lowered into place and temporarily bolted horizontally to its neighbors at either end and below, the jaws were deployed to their lowest position so that overlapping lines of rivet holes along the bottom length of the newly positioned plate could be hydraulically joined to the top of the existing one below. Six-foot-high plating was the rule; anything wider would have prevented the claws from reaching far enough down to encompass that essential depth of rivet line.

The convenience and efficiency of roofing a slipway with an overhead structure was, in fact, an American innovation, first perfected at Virginia's Newport News. Though one smaller overhead gantry had been erected above Harland and Wolff berths nos. 5 and 6, its design inspiration had also originated overseas, from the Brown Hoisting Machine Company of Cleveland, Ohio.

Other overseas deliveries for both *Olympic* and *Titanic* were turbines to drive their central propellers. They had been completed on order by engineers at Clydeside's rival yard John Brown. Having entered *Lusitania* into service in 1907, engineers at the Scottish yard had unquestionably emerged as the world's most skilled turbine fabricators. The machinery would be delivered from Clydeside to Belfast aboard a workhorse Harland and Wolff vessel called *Camel*, a specialized freighter with extra-large hatches giving access to deep holds with strengthened bottom plates. Curiously, rigged on her single mast, *Camel* also sported a large, gaff-rigged sail.

Extending Harland and Wolff's pervasive nepotism, former naval architect and now general manager Alexander Montgomery Carlisle was Lord Pirrie's brother-in-law. A benevolent, bearded Scot, known throughout the yard as "Big Alec," he would replicate past Harland and Wolff tonnage, adhering to the same reassuring lines of what had been informally described just after the turn of the century as White Star's "big four": *Celtic* and *Cedric* (1901 and 1903) followed by *Baltic* and *Adriatic* (1904 and 1907).

Their silhouettes were famous, Belfast classics sometimes described as coffin ships because of their flat bottoms and straight stems, designed for fast if not record-breaking speed. Their long, low-lying hulls were topped with twin stacks and four masts, their deep stern frames terminating in a shallow, cutaway counter. The topmost boat deck was conservatively designed, devoid of upwardly intruding glass domes save one forward topping the main staircase. Significantly, White Star almost never pursued the blue ribband. Save for *Teutonic* of 1899, there were no exceptions to the company's conservative building philosophy, a firm predilection that saw dispatch perennially subordinated to deluxe.

Though several of the "big four," as well as *Amerika*, built for Hamburg-America Line, would become, momentarily, the world's largest ships, all were effectively dwarfed by 1911's imposing new class. Yet in spite of *Olympic* and *Titanic*'s expanded displacement, Carlisle had ingeniously retained the archetypal simplicity established for the (now *not* so big) big four. Profiles of both *Olympic*-class ships avoided both the cumbersome instability of Hamburg-America Line's 1913 *Imperator* no less than the crowded top hamper of John Brown's *Aquitania*, which would enter service in the summer of 1914. Despite record-breaking displacement, Carlisle's latest vessels retained an endearing, yachtlike grace; given their monumental scale it was a remarkable naval architectural achievement.

At continental yards rudders were installed after launch, but both *Olympic*'s and *Titanic*'s rudders were installed prior. Seven attached gudgeons or round opening brackets lined rudder posts from top to bottom. Once the rudder had been maneuvered on chain hoists into position, each gudgeon was sited perfectly atop its opposite number, seven upward-pointing pintles riveted one above the other the height of the stern casting. After each pintle had penetrated the appropriate gudgeon the rudder could be lowered into place. Finishing touches were, first, capping the top of every protruding pintle with a heavy locking nut; then, in preparation for the rigors of the hull's stern-first entry into Belfast Lough, two pairs of strong flanking brackets, mounted one above the other, would lock the rudder firmly amidships. Those safety restraints would remain in place until their removal, months later, when the vessel was first dry-docked.

The *Olympic*-class rudders seemed small, given the vast dimensions of the hulls they adorned. But contemporary engineers and naval architects were at odds over the most efficacious rudder shape. For *Lusitania* and *Mauretania* it had been a far simpler matter. Both had to conform to the Admiralty's wartime specification of fully underwater balanced rudders, mandated to reduce vulnerability to hostile gunfire. Whereas *Olympic*-class vessels, because of their American ownership, faced no such strategic requirements, Sir William H. White, in his landmark *Manual of Naval Architecture* of 1900, suggested that White Star's rudder choice was similar to those used throughout the Royal Navy.

White espoused a rule of thumb based on hull/rudder proportions, suggesting that "the extreme breadth of the rudder [is often] from one-fortieth to one-sixtieth of the length." *Olympic* and *Titanic* just met those qualifications, their maximum rudder span of 15 feet (4.6 meters) being 1/57th the length of their 850-foot (259-meter) hull. Moreover, increasing the dimensions of *Titanic*'s rudder would have necessitated more powerful steering machinery.

Be that as it may, later tests with *Olympic* after *Titanic* foundered revealed that her rudder, identical to *Titanic*'s, offered a crucially slow turning moment: a glacial 37 seconds elapsed between tiller command and hull response.

Harland and Wolff launches were exciting yet underplayed, compared to those in other yards. Neither celebratory godmother nor breaking champagne were involved. But both J. P. Morgan and Bruce Ismay were in attendance, as were a hundred thousand lesser Belfast mortals. In his element, Lord Pirrie officiated. On

20 October 1910, after two warning red rockets had been sent up to clear shipping from the launch path, *Olympic*'s hull, its triggers released, slid flawlessly into sight, emerging from beneath its gantry and plunging triumphantly into Belfast Lough.

Once she had been maneuvered alongside the fitting-out pier and secured, first priority was installation of large engine parts. Components of two huge four-cylinder, triple-expansion reciprocating engines were raised up from workshop flatbed cars that had delivered them from prolonged bench testing in the engine works. They were hoisted aloft by a giant floating crane from Germany called Hercules, a secondhand purchase that had been towed across both the North Sea and the Irish Sea to Belfast. Every massive engine increment went aboard—twenty-nine double-ended boilers, condensers, generators, and Scottish turbines—lowered one by one through the vessel's open casings on wind-free days, manhandled into position before being attached to stout foundation plates riveted firmly atop the double bottoms.

Having agreed with Bruce Ismay to build his record-breaking vessels, Pirrie had financed construction of the requisite twin slipways and their covering gantries. Though he had made no provision for constructing a dry dock for the new class, he obtained one at no cost thanks to some shameless blackmail. With the arrogance for which he was famous, Pirrie insisted that Belfast's Harbour Commission undertake construction of a dry dock at the commission's expense. If he was refused, Pirrie, exercising the same blunt tactics with which his predecessor had defied nascent unionists, threatened to relocate Harland and Wolff elsewhere. It was more than an idle boast, for he made clear that a search for suitable real estate was already under way in both Liverpool and along the Clyde.

Most worrisome to the commission was the prospect of Belfast losing 43,000 jobs; its hand was forced. Funds were allocated, a site for the dry dock was cleared, and work began. The Thompson

Graving Dock was the result, named after Robert Thompson, Belfast alderman and Harbour Commission member who had seen the wisdom of acceding to Pirrie's demand.

The world's largest graving dock at the time of its construction, it was 900 feet long, comfortably in excess of *Olympic*'s 850-foot length between perpendiculars and wider than her 92-foot beam. Although Harland and Wolff's famous berths nos. 2 and 3 have long since vanished, the Thompson Graving Dock still exists, together with the preserved shell of its adjacent pump house. The two remain one of the increasingly rare surviving elements of the yard's 1912 infrastructure.

The dock had been excavated and lined in traditional fashion. Halfway up from the dock floor, stepped granite sides provided bracing points for long, squared oak shores with terminal iron collars, to keep the hull firmly and vertically upright as the dock drained. Below those stepped levels additional shores could be accommodated, if necessary, within a horizontal line of square holes perforating the length of the masonry walls.

The Thompson Graving Dock began operation on 1 April 1911, its first occupant RMS *Olympic*. Second of the class *Titanic* would undergo an identical dry-docking, duplicating that of the first without exception.

Perhaps the dock's most novel feature was its primitive method of admitting and exiting hulls. Since there was no room inside for accompanying tugs, the business of maneuvering *Olympic* into and out of the dock depended, as did so much at Harland and Wolff, on brute manual labor. Centered at the inland end of the dock was a massive yellow-and-black capstan, its iron base sunk more than a dozen feet into a stout cement footing. Its revolving iron head accommodated eight projecting keys or bars, around which a force of sixteen men could plod in a hard-fought circle. From *Olympic*'s bow, positioned by tugs and waiting just outside the dock, a long hawser had been rove through her fairlead—the towing aperture atop the stem—and laid the length of the dock before being secured with five turns round the capstan.

Sixteen men pushing those capstan bars would provide the muscle to bring the world's largest vessel into the dock. It turned easily at first, the retaining pawls clacking as increasing tension raised the hawser from underwater before squeezing lines of water droplets from the tautening hemp.

Then the brutal work started. As the foreman barked encouragement, the brawny workmen put their backs into it, heaving and straining in dogged unison, each pair intent on inching their wooden bar forward. The hardest labor came at the start, overcoming the 45,000-ton hull's inertia. But once the vessel stirred and started a grudging move, *Olympic* was slowly winched inside, moving at a majestic snail's pace closer and closer to the revolving capstan.

Long before that entry, before the dock was flooded, *Olympic*'s docking plan had been implemented, a fixed pattern of keel blocks laid out with exquisite care along the dock floor. Each iron block was made up of interlocking components stacked one atop the other. Protecting the hull from that unforgiving metal were insulating wooden slabs of iroko, an extremely hard and water-resilient African tree.

As the Thompson Graving Dock is preserved today, too many iron blocks are parked along the center line as a storage expedient, far more than *Olympic* would have required. Since the vessel's frames were on 36-inch (91 centimeters) centers amidships and 24-inch (61 centimeters) centers at each narrowing end of the hull, the docking plan required that keel blocks beneath the main part of the hull be set a scrupulous yard apart; at either end, they were denser, closed up for 2-foot centers.

Positioning the hull precisely was essential. Each interior ship's frame had to settle perfectly atop a block. Were a block to project upward *between* frames, *Olympic*'s bottom plating might have been dimpled. During the procedure, oak shores were rigged, laid horizontally between hull and stepped dock walls, one end wedged tight against *Olympic*'s shell plating, the other parked snugly on the appropriate granite level, ensuring rigid verticality.

Because of spatial limitations to either side of the graving dock's entrance, there was no room for a sliding gate to exclude the waters of Abercorn Basin. Instead, the entry would be blocked by a movable, rectangular plug, of exactly the same dimension as the opening; the plug was hollow and could be filled with water to increase its weight. Once *Olympic* had been correctly positioned and secured, the empty, buoyant caisson was detached from its parking bollards outside the entrance and maneuvered into position, floating directly above the dock's threshold. Then it was flooded, sinking down onto the sill to close the entrance, its surrounding margins sealed with crushed peat.

Even though *Olympic* was now in exact position and the caisson closed, the docking foreman still did not signal engineers inside the pump house to drain the dock. Essential rail deliveries were due on the looped spur of railway track encircling the dock. That trackage had been snugged as close as possible to dock's edge so that steam cranes mounted atop flatbed cars would be in prime position for lowering deliveries straight down to the dock floor.

Interspersed between steam cranes were flatbeds loaded with equipment essential for dry docking, including more than two dozen flat-bottomed scows, each laden with a consignment of long-handled scrapers and wire-bristled scrubbers. This was the first time *Olympic*'s hull had been out of water since her October launch the previous year. Accumulated barnacles and growth had to be scoured from her underwater plating by men working from those scows as the water level receded. Scrupulously clean bottom plating was a prerequisite for both painting and subsequent sea trials.

When the dock was dry, grounded scows were removed one by one, hoisted up with workers still aboard, their last free ride. Thereafter, they would achieve the dock floor via one of six descents. Two were on either side of the dock entrance, conventional railed staircases leading down on either side of *Olympic*'s stern. Four additional descents flanked the length of the dock, two a side: steep slopes cut through the masonry walls. All four had been constructed with two parallel paths, one a slide, the other a staircase. Men first slid their tools, lashed inside canvas bags, down the slope before jumping onto the slide themselves, tempering their speed of descent by bracing boots against either iron side. Their reverse journey at quitting time was more demanding. Shouldering tool bags, they started a long climb up the accompanying cement staircases to ground level, emerging like subway passengers along the dock margins.

Olympic's propellers were the next items delivered from the works. However formidable that majestic profile had seemed during entry, the vessel was still navigationally impotent that first April morn of 1911, lacking motive elements beneath her counter. Tail shafts were in place, already flanged onto the main shafts installed during construction. Now propelling elements were lowered from delivering flatbeds onto the graving dock floor by the train's skilled crane operators.

The trio of propellers driving *Olympic*-class ships differed. Outboard, an identical pair of three-bladed propellers were shafted to the largest steam reciprocating engines ever installed in a liner. Their leftover steam would power the Clydeside turbines that would rotate a single, four-bladed propeller positioned along the keel line. The disadvantage of that central propeller—the built-in trap of every odd-numbered screw total—was its obligatory central placement, prohibiting deployment of a larger and more efficient balanced rudder.

Once these components had been lowered to the bottom of the graving dock, each could thereafter be raised by muscle power only, using lines suspended from "rabbit ears"—steel brackets permanently riveted onto the fantail underside of *Olympic*'s overhanging counter stern. Those sky hooks would remain permanently in place for the life of the vessel, essential adjuncts for every dry-docking.

Thankfully, the three blades of port and starboard reciprocating engine propellers were separate and detachable. Dock workers sweating at chain hoists and block and tackles first raised and attached each propeller hub. Once that central boss had been married to protruding tail shaft, successive blades could be lifted up and bolted in place. Final attachment was a conical steel cap, covering and finishing the entire assembly.

The central propeller, driven by the newfangled turbine, had all four blades permanently attached, a sculpted, manganese-bronze casting that had been poured within a laboriously wrought, brick-lined cement mold at Harland and Wolff. After it had cooled for ten days, the outer negative mold was shattered; among the rubble lay the crude bronze casting. Only after polishing and balancing could it be delivered to the graving dock.

Installing that central propeller on the keel line was a finicky and demanding procedure. The complete propeller had to be coaxed athwartship, to hang inside what was, in effect, a vertical steel window, its forward margin the skeg or after-end of the keel, and the opposite one the rudder stem casting. Chain hoists from both port and starboard sky hooks had to be attached and later interchanged, coaxing the propeller inside its framed aperture before it could be nudged forward onto the tail shaft. Much patient juggling was required before it was finally attached and locked in place. Only then were the chain hoists detached, allowing a third conical cap to be mounted, completing that final screw's assembly.

While that vital work around the stern was under way, the same teams of men that had scraped and scrubbed the underwater hull plates clambered up ladders with paint and brushes to cover *Olympic*'s shell plating with successive layers of black or—below water descending from what was called the boot topping—carmine anti-corrosive paint. In today's dry docks, paint-brushes have been outmoded; hull paint is sprayed on instead, faster and more efficiently. But circa 1911 traditional hand painting remained the yard's only recourse. Wide hand brushes were dipped repeatedly into paint cans and slathered along the steel by men atop a framework of cobbled-together ladders and scaffolding rising from the dry dock floor. Other painters, in that puddled, claustrophobic netherworld beneath the hull, stooped or just sat atop overturned paint cans, daubing the bottom plates above their paint-splattered heads.

After the paint had dried and the work on *Olympic*'s after end completed, the graving dock floor was evacuated of scaffolding, ladders, brushes, and empty paint cans and the pump house machinery activated to flood it. Hawsers attached to the vessel's stern bits were rove around a pair of capstans, situated to either side of the dock exit. A single capstan could not be used because there was no way to erect a central pulling source directly astern of the hull out in Abercorn Basin; it would have conflicted with the emerging hull's vector.

When the flooded dock's water level achieved parity with exterior Abercorn Basin the caisson was pumped out to achieve buoyancy, floated off the sill, and maneuvered by tugs back into parking position along the dock's eastern side. Then, as teams of workmen struggled around port and starboard capstans—their toil made easier by their halved burden—*Olympic* was drawn slowly out of the dock toward waiting shipyard tugs that would maneuver her back alongside the fitting-out pier. Still, things were not easy; those circling the westernmost capstan risked tripping over intruding rails and ties of the dock's delivery track, across which they stumbled during every hard-fought circuit.

The painters daubing the hull either atop scaffolding or beneath it lacked the skill of specialized painters later deployed on scaffolding suspended over the vessel's sides. Those more skilled men would implement a decorative golden flourish surrounding the entire hull at the level of the strength deck. California artist Ken Marschall, who has devoted years of intense study to the *Olympic*-class vessels, shared some historic details about that gold stripe. It was not, as Geoffrey Marcus's *The Maiden Voyage* suggests, gold leaf, but a primrose yellow paint, adulterated with a greenish tinge that aped gold leaf. That distinctive stripe encircling *Titanic*'s hull was lower than it had been on *Olympic*, positioned at what Harland and Wolff elevation plans called the sheer line, just beneath C Deck's porthole line rather than B Deck's strength deck.

Hulls adorned with racing stripes are demanding to maintain and would become even harder aboard *Olympic* after World War I. As part of her famous makeover in the 1920s, her racing stripe was lowered so that it was no longer merely a yellow border separating black hull from white superstructure but a 10¼-inch-wide (26 centimeters) yellow band delineated by black, with both upper and lower cutting lines requiring maintenance. Further complicating matters, the stripe tapered as it approached the bow.

The same yellow hue was used for the *Olympic*-class vessels' three painted names: one each on port and starboard bows and one surrounding the counter aft, where it also incorporated port of registry LIVERPOOL. Marschall deduced from surviving tender *Nomadic's* name treatment as well as examination of the vessel's plating remnants at the bottom of the Atlantic that it was not Harland and Wolff practice to attach steel cut letters. Instead, artisans impressed or lightly engraved each letter's outline as well as the stripe margins a few millimeters into the steel as a guide; that depth kept it visible despite accumulating layers of paint.

Just as those exterior adornments enriched the *Olympic*-class hulls, Thomas Andrews also pulled out all the stops for their passenger appointments inside. Although private bathrooms were still rare aboard Edwardian tonnage, Andrews had implemented some ingeniously designed ones for both *Olympic* and *Titanic* by creation of intermediate spaces between his best B deck cabins. Slightly less generous than the cabin widths, every rectangular sanitary block was divided by a diagonal wall that created two adjacent private bathrooms. Each pair was shaped like interlocked grand pianos: the broader "keyboard" end accommodated the fore-and-aft length of a tub, while the opposite narrow end housed an enclosed toilet. Sinks were hung on either side of the dividing wall.

For *Titanic*, Andrews upgraded the vessel's most lavish cabins even more. *Olympic*'s lower-level supplementary promenades were dispensed with, supplanted by expanded cabin walls that Andrews pushed all the way out to the vessel's sides. He created his most splendiferous suites at the forward end of those amplified quarters. There were only two, one on each side. On the starboard side, three adjoining cabins—B-51, B-53, and B-55—were fashioned into two bedrooms, a communicating bath, and a sitting room, complete with faux fireplace. Extended out toward the ship's side, incorporating the width of all three combined cabins, was a spacious (and unique) private promenade.

The *Olympic*-class's most appealing public rooms were the A la Carte dining rooms, White Star's first experimentation with extra-tariff restaurants. Both were located aft on B Deck on the frontier separating first from second, directly beneath the vessel's fourth dummy funnel. All that vented through that monumental buff-colored fake were negligible turbine room fumes and A la Carte galley smoke.

Because of its borderline location, *Olympic*'s original A la Carte bow windows looked out either side onto flanking second class promenades; had they not been discreetly curtained, first class clientele not only would have gazed at second class strollers but also would have been stared at in return.

But not for long. Once the prototypical A la Carte was unveiled aboard *Olympic*'s June 1911 maiden, its immediate popularity ensured that the room and its adjacent galley would be expanded, a larger footprint reflected from the beginning aboard *Titanic*. The port walls of *Olympic*'s original restaurant and galley were displaced outboard to the side of the vessel, co-opting and truncating the (always expendable) promenading space of an inferior class. There was forward creep as well, requiring the demolition of two first class cabins to permit enlargement of the galley. Because Andrews's lateral cabin expansion had obliterated *Titanic*'s B Deck promenade, passengers bound for the restaurant could achieve it only via the aftermost staircase.

On the starboard side, the (former) second class promenade was now enclosed inside a stylish treillage interior combining breakfast, lunch, and café offerings as well as a de facto waiting room called the Café Parisian. Here was more White Star–fractured French: though labeled with the adjective correctly succeeding the noun, deck plans retained the Gallic inversion but embraced English-spelled "Parisian."

The café's inboard wall still incorporated the same bow window that had pierced both of the original restaurant's flanking bulkheads. On *Olympic*, a windproof revolving door gave admittance, preventing intruding sea breezes that otherwise would have scoured the restaurant with every entry. Aboard *Titanic*, where promenade deck breezes had been negated by Andrews's cabin extensions, a revolving door was unnecessary; entry into the restaurant was achieved from the after staircase landing.

Decoration of the A la Carte restaurant adhered, as did so many *Olympic*-class interiors, to the elegant vernacular of Louis XVI. Just as the popular Edwardian composer Archibald Joyce would give his bittersweet waltz "Songe d'Automne" a French name, the same Gallic pretension consumed Harland and Wolff's interior designers. The space was paneled in French walnut, the walls divided into oval cartouches that were either mirrored or accented with carved, gilded ribbon bands and looping garlands of fruit. Domed glass Lightolier fixtures marched across the ceiling, while underfoot pink-patterned Axminster carpeting prevailed. Every table had its own lamp and the flower arrangements were, inevitably, a mix of carnations and daisies, renowned in the catering trade for maximum longevity. Columns skewering every serving station were fluted walnut, enriched by further gilt banding. We know exactly how *Olympic*'s A la Carte paneling looked, because against all odds much of it has been restored and installed today as decor for the Olympic restaurant aboard the Celebrity cruise ship *Millennium*.

In its earliest configuration aboard *Olympic*, the restaurant occupied a rectangle 62 feet (19 meters) wide and 38 feet (12 meters) long. Within those 2,356 square feet (212 square meters), 99 customers rejoiced in spacious comfort. But when the restaurant was expanded, cover numbers were increased to 168; and with requisite furniture added the layout became denser, as it would also be aboard *Titanic*. One maître d'hôtel, two headwaiters, fourteen waiters, and sixteen assistant waiters had to ply their trade with scant room to maneuver. The bar, so called, was really an elaborate sideboard positioned along the forward wall, too small for any good use; its solitary barman could only deliver aperitifs to diners or their successors waiting out in the Café Parisian.

Beyond the green baize door, working conditions in pantry, galley, and scullery were, at best, hectic. Though all three had been enlarged, additional specialized cubbyholes took up the slack:

an expanded wine store, a chef's office, a separate fish store, space for fruit and flowers, another office for controller and cashiers, extra dishwashers, and, perhaps the coolest job in that frenetic hotbox, a solitary iceman.

The galley workforce, twenty-five sous-chefs and *aides-de-cuisine* under Chef Pierre Rousseau, had been almost exclusively recruited from London's Oddenino's Imperial Restaurant. Suiting kitchen staffing protocol of the period, each sauce, roast, pastry, fish, and entrée cook was assigned his own assistant, jostling for elbow room within a tight-packed venue. In the pantry, noisily adjacent to the dining room, four dishwashers—two for plates, two for glasses—toiled shoulder to shoulder with three scullery men scouring a clangor of pots and pans.

The restaurant entry was equally crowded. Enlarging *Olympic*'s restaurant had necessitated demolition of two three-berth cabins on the starboard side to allow for creation of an amplified wine cellar and coat-check alcove. Also, space had to be found for a piano trio. Unable to play *inside* the restaurant—not one square inch was available—they were tucked instead into a corner of the staircase landing, with room only for an upright piano. Those A la Carte musicians on both ships serenaded their clientele only during entry. In fact, their music may well have attracted future clients who could not but help overhear their seductive musical strains wafting up or down the after staircase.

Those A la Carte lunches and dinners were not the fixed, obligatory sittings of the main dining saloon but, inevitably, longer gatherings. For dinners especially, customers had booked for a festive night out, away from assigned seats. The convivial chatter of preferred tablemates meant lengthier meals that sabotaged management's profit-driven turnover rate. As a result, it was hard to predict how many covers (and their revenue) could be scheduled of an evening.

The same dilemma plagues every extra-tariff shipboard operation, anathema to maîtres d'hôtel who, having enthusiastically booked successive passenger parties, often have to stack them, like incoming aircraft circling above crowded airports. They were kept waiting in the Café Parisian where they tapped their feet, less in time to the music than increasingly impatient to dine.

Before we leave Belfast, it must be said. Two bright yellow gantries, giant inverted steel U's initialed *H W* and nicknamed by Belfast's natives "Samson and Goliath," still tower over what once was the working shipyard Harland and Wolff. They no longer stir because the place has been deactivated and closed down for several years, its workforce dispersed, its shops, dry docks, and sheds emptied and in the process of being demolished.

The sprawling acreage has been bought by Norwegian shipping magnate Fred Olsen. His is not a maritime but a real estate investment. And catering to an apparently unstoppable worldwide interest in *Titanic*, what remains of that vast shipbuilding legacy is in the process of—dread word—development. Of actual restoration, there is none, save for the financially deprived renovation of White Star's salvaged Cherbourg tender *Nomadic*, rescued from Parisian exile as a Japanese restaurant moored in the Seine.

Elsewhere, there is spurious reproduction aplenty but no preservation. Indeed, every day there is less and less to preserve. Typical of today's Harland and Wolff are several bulldozed rearrangements of the yard's stalwart origins. Once-straight Queen's Road has been rewrought with curves "for interest"; rising next to it is a £120 million *Titanic* Museum, a two-building, glass-fronted complex with side walls sloping inward to suggest the sheer of White Star hull plating; farther along Queen's Road, the great drawing office with its distinctive domed skylight is being gentrified into a boutique hotel; Samson and Goliath are rumored to be up for sale, available for removal and reerection elsewhere in the shipbuilding world.

Even the historic Thompson Graving Dock is at risk. There is talk that the dock floor will be "enriched" with an illuminated replica of *Titanic*'s hull, in effect tarting up a peerless original with a spurious overlay.

Belfast's and Fred Olsen's combined strategy is as clear as it is inescapable. No financial return can be derived from a moribund industrial site. Attracting visitors and their cash to Belfast requires carefully planned titillation, creation of what is fast becoming a *Titanic* theme park.

I only wish I had undertaken research for this book earlier, while Harland and Wolff was still a valid, working entity. Nowadays, visiting historians encounter only twenty-first-century replications of vanished Edwardian actuality. The ground floor of the graving dock pump house, for instance, has been revamped into a tourist shop, awash with souvenir postcards, dish towels, key chains, and pen-and-pencil sets, merchandise offered to visiting school groups with restricted funds, allowing them to take home reminders, if not actual remnants, of *Titanic*. Refreshments are available as well, the predictable cycle of shopping and snacking in lugubrious train.

In sum, Harland and Wolff is on the road to becoming yet another kind of Disneyland. Hornblow at Queen's Island has been dumbed down; the throaty shriek of the yard's original steam whistle has degenerated into the bland tin horn of the marketing huckster.

In early April of 1912 *Titanic* left Belfast for Southampton. We should do the same, following her route to the great port on Britain's south coast where ambitious preparations had been in train since 1908 to create adequate docks and dry docks for White Star's overwhelming new class of ocean liner.

CHAPTER 4

THE OCEAN DOCK

There goes old Captain Smith again, trying for third time unlucky! He's already had two collisions!

Crewman chortling to his mate as *New York* drifts toward outbound *Titanic* in Southampton

The Titanic *sank at 2:20 this morning. No lives were lost.*

Reuters dispatch, 15 April 1912

Arriving in Southampton aboard Queen Mary 2 in summer 2009, I was delighted to discover, belatedly, that the port's most historic body of water had been restored to passenger use after a twenty-five-year intermission. It was both surprising and somehow remarkable to tie up again in the Ocean Dock. For years, both *Queen Elizabeth 2* and *Queen Mary 2* had routinely moored farther down the dock peninsula at the Queen Elizabeth II terminal (named after the monarch, not the vessel). Sometimes they still do; on our second 2009 call, we disembarked there again, even though the newly restored facility was vacant.

The Ocean Dock is irrevocably linked with *Titanic*. First excavated in 1908 by the dockland's owner, the London and Southwestern Railway Company, it was a vital adjunct to accommodate the anticipated *Olympic*-class giants. That those huge vessels were to sail from the port was a feather in the city's cap, inaugurating Southampton's golden age. Shortly after the turn of the century it became Britain's preferred transatlantic terminus, closer to London than Liverpool, connected by a fast railway line constructed in 1840.

Since Roman times, Southampton has boasted a singular navigational advantage: its double tide. As ebbing waters slip down-Channel, portions of its flow are diverted northward by the Isle of Wight's Ryde peninsula, inundating Southampton Water with an intermediate flood. That unique, deepwater availability was a vast improvement over the cumbersome up-Mersey ordeal to reach Liverpool's landing stage.

That advantage was and still is offset by an annoying shoal obstructing the dock approaches. Southampton lies at the mouth of the Itchen and Test, two south-flowing rivers that drain much of Hampshire. Bracketing the dock peninsula before merging just south of it, their combined waters proceed down relatively narrow Southampton Water until it broadens into its triangular confluence with the Solent and Spithead. Because of that broadening, the rivers' current slows and masses of carried silt, thus far held in suspension en route to the Channel, drop to the bottom, creating a huge mudflat.

Like a cork in a bottle that mudflat has been there for years, christened the Brambles. Never was a hazard better named—a clutching, thorny growth ensnaring unwary passersby. To circumvent it, all in- and outbound traffic must follow the circumventing Thorn Channel, a tortuous reverse-S detour.

The most vexing aspect of the Brambles is that it defies remedy. Neither reef nor rocky outcrop that can be blasted clear, it is a constantly growing depth of mud. Were dredges set to work, deposits of Test and Itchen silt would continue to accumulate, replacing laboriously excavated spoil.

Whenever passenger vessels stray from the Thorn Channel and run afoul of the Brambles, they are held aground until the rising tide and, inevitably, a host of tugs breaks them loose from the mud suction of their unwanted perch. There is seldom hull damage, merely embarrassment and expensive delays of docking and sailing schedules. Victims have included *Majestic* and *Aquitania* in the thirties, postwar *Ile de France* and the first *Queen Elizabeth* in 1947, and even *QE2* inbound from New York just before her departure for Dubai retirement.

When seasonal tides are low, that mudflat actually emerges above water. Uffa Fox, the late Cowes yachtsman, pioneered annual Brambles cricket matches. Because of the imminent flood, innings were always brief, made sometimes briefer if anyone clouted the ball into deep water, thereby canceling play.

The Brambles aside, departures from and arrivals at England's south coast put British tonnage in prime competition with continental rivals across the Channel and North Sea. However remote from Liverpool, French, Dutch, German, and Scandinavian steamers were close to Southampton. All of them used the port as a convenient way station for picking up or depositing UK passengers.

White Star was not the first company to start forsaking Liverpool. Once the American Line had bought the bankrupt Inman Line in 1893, it instigated the first southward migration to Southampton. White Star followed suit in 1907 when three company stalwarts—*Teutonic*, *Majestic*, and *Oceanic*—were repositioned there, establishing a weekly service from the port to New York. Their relatively modest size enabled them to be moored within the Empress Dock, an eighteen-and-a-half-acre enclosed facility on the dock peninsula's eastern side that Queen Victoria had opened in 1890. Cunard stayed put in Liverpool until after World War I when heavyweights *Mauretania*, *Aquitania*, and *Berengaria* became Southampton regulars as well.

In addition to offering adequate berthing space and swift communication with the capital, successful transatlantic ports had also to provide adequate dry docking. Southampton had met that requirement with construction of the Prince of Wales Graving Dock of 1895, opened by His Royal Highness five years after his mother had done the honors for the Empress Dock.

Three years earlier, when the London and South Western Railway company took over ownership of the port from the bankrupt Southampton Dock company, its managing director announced proudly that the port could now receive the "world's largest steamers." But hyperbole of that kind was ill-advised once Edwardian shipbuilders began pushing the tonnage envelope. When the Prince of Wales Graving Dock proved too small, a larger Trafalgar Graving Dock was gouged out of the peninsula to the west. Only 875 feet long and 90 feet wide (205 × 27 meters), it would not accommodate *Olympic*'s 882½-foot overall length and beam of 92 feet. Fortunately, there is an expensive and time-consuming way to amplify a too-small dry dock by reexcavating one long wall and carving a bow notch in the center of its inland masonry, into which *Olympic*'s forepeak could be snugged. It was completed in 1905.

Although the amended Trafalgar Dock took care of dry docking, creation of an adequate wet dock was urgently required. *Olympic*-class vessels could not possibly berth in the outmoded Empress Dock. A huge, new facility would have to be excavated between just completed Trafalgar Dock and the dock peninsula. During its construction and working life, it would be identified by four successive names: officially the Deep Water Ocean Dock, immediately abbreviated to Ocean Dock; the Sixteen-Acre Dock (in fact, only fifteen and a half acres of water are enclosed); and the White Star Dock, a press favorite paying lip service to the line that had mandated its creation.

Construction of the Ocean Dock completed the distinctive, arrowhead footprint of Southampton's dock peninsula. That latest facility, a perfect parallelogram, remained wide open to the waters of the river Test flowing past its entrance. A diagonal slash cut through the riverbank—the parallelogram's watery threshold—was 400 feet (121 meters) wide, exactly the width of the slips separating Manhattan's finger piers. In the parallelogram's inland

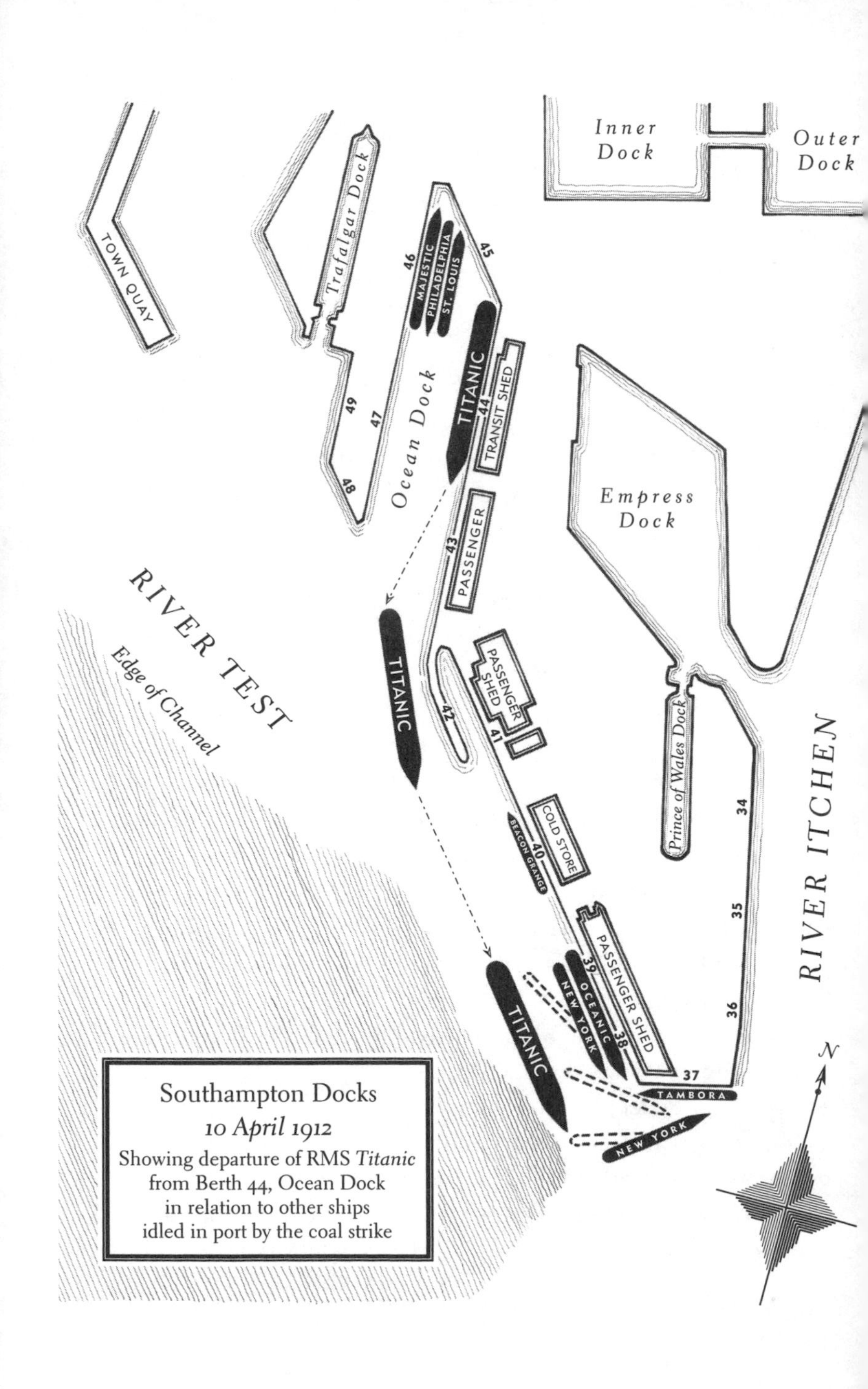

Southampton Docks
10 April 1912
Showing departure of RMS *Titanic*
from Berth 44, Ocean Dock
in relation to other ships
idled in port by the coal strike

peak, floating rubbish blown into the dock accumulates, detritus that has fouled that watery apex for years.

Each of the dock's long sides was 1,600 feet (485 meters), nearly long enough to accommodate a brace of *Olympics*. Postwar, giant steamship quartets routinely filled it. Once, in the early 1920s, *Mauretania* and *Adriatic* lay bow to stern along its eastern side, an easily accommodated aggregate of 1,200 feet (364 meters). But across the way *Berengaria* and *Aquitania*, at 884 feet and 869 feet, respectively, took up 1,753 feet (531 meters) of berthing space, exceeding the dock's length. *Aquitania*'s stern jutted out into the Test, just the way *Olympic*'s had extended into the Hudson during her maiden berthing at New York's Pier 59.

No sheltering jetties extended into the stream, allowing the Ocean Dock to breathe, so to speak, with the combined ship lengths to which it periodically played host. Their absence, alas, leaves the entrance vulnerable to Test silt, which continually meanders inside. But there was a convenient extension sheltering the eastern entrance, a hook-shaped coaling pier that served two purposes: providing a protective niche for ships' bows loading either coal or timber and, along its gently curving outer wall, a benevolent knuckle against which inbound hulls could be turned if necessary.

Ocean Dock's most critical dimension was its depth, 40 feet (12.1 meters) at low water, leaving a comfortable 5-foot margin below *Olympic*'s keel. The two original *Queens* had whopping drafts of 42 feet (12.7 meters), obliging them to await high water before entering. Modern-day cruise ships require less depth; even *Queen Mary 2* 's draft is only 32 feet (9.7 meters). Nevertheless, whenever she enters the dock its waters are tainted by clouds of roiled mud.

After flowing past the Ocean Dock, the river Test's course parallels the docks' western flank. Every berth surrounding that peninsula is numbered, starting with berth no. 1 from the earliest Inner Docks. Nowadays Inner, Outer, and Empress docks have all been filled in but the original numbering system remains as was. Today, surviving berths no. 34, no. 35, and no. 36 line the peninsula's eastern side, laved by the river Itchen. Situated around the peninsula's flattened tip is berth no. 37. Turning north in Test country, a long passenger shed occupied berths nos. 38 and 39; next, Europe's largest cold storage facility filled berth no. 40 and another passenger shed lay along berth no. 41; berth no. 42 was the hooked coaling pier's exterior side.

Entering Ocean Dock, numbering continues counterclockwise around the parallelogram's three dry sides. Occupying its eastern expanse, a passenger shed filled berth no. 43, so too neighboring no. 44. Berth no. 45 lay along the parallelogram's abbreviated inland dimension, while berths nos. 46 and 47 took up the long western side. Back out beside the Test was another short berth, no. 48. Past it, and northward around the corner, berth no. 49 ended at the Trafalgar Graving Dock's seaward caisson.

Of all those numbers, it is berth no. 44—farthest inland on the parallelogram's eastern side—that most concerns us. This was the location of what we must call Ocean Terminal I, transfer point linking boat train passengers from Waterloo with the enormous hulls awaiting them in Ocean Dock. It was a practical if architecturally undistinguished structure, nothing more than two parallel workaday train sheds with a 700-foot frontage, shorter than *Olympic*'s hull but sufficiently commodious inside. On a decorative par with New York's utilitarian pier sheds, it boasted no interior cladding whatsoever. Exposed steel trusses supported the terminal's doubled roof ridges and movable wooden railings funneled inbound passengers past port officials' desks.

Southampton's tidal range is far more modest than Liverpool's so no floating landing stages—Mersey essentials that rose and fell at the same time as the vessels moored to their seaward sides—were necessary. Instead, dock engineers coped with Southampton tides with two double-decked gantries, nothing more than windowed, wheeled boxes 20 feet (6 meters) wide and 40 feet tall. Their floor levels were identical save for their height above ground. Depending on the tide, either could deliver cabin passengers directly into *Olympic*'s appropriate hull openings. First class passengers trooped aboard forward, second class near the stern, while, perhaps predictably, steerage passengers were denied shelter of any kind.

Along the 35-foot (10.6 meter) cement apron separating berth no. 44's margin from the Ocean Terminal's facade, three sets of rails were placed in the concrete. Outboard, the largest had one track positioned right along the dock's edge, permitting the movement of advanced, electrically operated cranes. As they moved along the dock, a large retaining wheel of power cable unspooled into a gutter specifically dug for the purpose. Between the overall span of those crane tracks were two more rails, along which dockworkers shifted by hand the aforementioned gantries. The final set of tracks was of standard railway gauge so goods trains could unload alongside the hulls to provision the ships. Boat trains never used that dockside apron but arrived and departed out of sight, drawing up to covered platforms paralleling the terminal's inland wall.

A replacement Ocean Terminal was erected after World War II. The first had become a victim of not only age but also German bombs; additionally, the debut of larger steamers mandated an entirely new and larger facility. Ocean Dock frontage had to be amplified and consolidated to accommodate the 1,000-foot (303 meters) *Queens*, Cunard's two-ship weekly mail service to New York. Those floating benchmarks required a longer and more ambitious terminal.

Architectural pretension neglected for prewar Ocean Terminal I materialized in spades for Ocean Terminal II. A giant art deco glass-and-steel structure, it consumed and combined berths nos. 43 and 44. It was 1,297 feet (393 meters) long, mimicking, in size and form, the vessels it served. The imposing southern facade greeting inbound traffic was topped by a semicircular glass tower, apparent land-based simulacrum of a *Queen*'s bridge screen. Outbound passengers, descending from concealed boat train platforms along the terminal's rear walls, stepped onto escalators that carried them up through successive levels of handsomely finished interiors. They would embark aboard the *Queens* through enclosed, tubular gangways. First conceived in the 1920s and finally unveiled by Prime Minister Clement Attlee in July 1950, the new structure enriched and transformed the entire length of the Ocean Dock's eastern margin.

It welcomed other vessels in addition to the two *Queens*. I last sailed from Ocean Dock on *Norway*-ex-*France*'s maiden voyage to New York in May 1980. Three years later it closed down. By then, both postwar *Queens* were long gone, one to Long Beach retirement, the other to fiery destruction in Hong Kong. There was talk that the terminal might become a broadcasting facility for Southern Television but the plan was never implemented. After thirty-three years' use the structure was demolished. Its only surviving relics were stainless steel letters spelling out OCEAN TERMINAL on the facade, which ended up with American collectors; the SOUTHAMPTON letters encircling the topmost tower disappeared.

With Ocean Terminal II destroyed, the raison d'être of the Ocean Dock was destroyed as well. Passenger service was abrogated in favor of freight. Rather than ocean liners, car carriers, tankers, and freighters tied up there instead and, for a long time, its eastern margin was despoiled by a towering heap of scrap metal so large that the dock was in danger of collapsing.

Today, back in the business for which it had originally been designed, Ocean Dock regularly plays host to *Queens Mary 2*, *Vic-*

toria, and *Elizabeth* as well as rival cruising tonnage. Their passengers embark from or disembark into Ocean Terminal III. This is no retro art deco installation but, built by Cunard's owner, the Carnival Corporation, seems a squat, aluminum-paneled bunker, its domed roof and adjacent shelter faintly reminiscent of a flying saucer.

Perhaps the most surprising thing about Ocean Terminal III is that it encompasses berths no. 46 and no. 47 on the dock's *western* side, directly opposite the site of both predecessors. Obviously, the decision to erect it there was based on traffic logistics because almost all of today's dockland transportation embraces road instead of rail; only a single tracked spur still extends south as far as the Queen Elizabeth II terminal. But rather than shunting boat trains it is crowded with double-decked, covered goods wagons laden with Jaguar automobiles for export.

Not only has most of the docks' trackage disappeared beneath asphalt, even the historic railed interface between the capital and Southampton's docks is no more. London boat trains—traditional and inescapable adjuncts to every voyage in or out of the port—have disappeared. Like too many short-haul rail journeys throughout the UK, track has been superseded by road. Though privatized British Rail still offers excellent long-haul service between London and Scotland, the traditional ninety-minute run connecting Waterloo with Southampton's docks has been subsumed by charabancs. These days, to achieve a vessel from the capital, forget the boat train; struggle aboard a "boat bus" instead.

Placement of Ocean Terminal III on the Ocean Dock's western flank capitalizes on extensive parking space, including broad asphalt approaches for cars, taxis, and buses. Much of that additional macadam rests atop poor old Trafalgar Graving Dock. Only the dock's entrance sill remains; the rest has been filled in and paved over. Had Ocean Terminal III adopted the location of its predecessors, accommodating that vehicular traffic would have been impossible. The archetypal, modern-day cruise terminal that dominates Miami, Fort Lauderdale, Tampa, and Cape Canaveral, Florida, and, most recently, Brooklyn's Red Hook has spread its sprawling imprint to Britain's busiest passenger port.

But in addition to traffic patterns, did anyone consider weather patterns? Though Ocean Terminal III's location capitalizes on expanded vehicular capacity, there remains the nagging problem of Southampton's prevailing winds. All year they blow consistently out of the southwest. As a result, passenger vessels moored on the Ocean Dock's western margin endure almost constant offshore thrust. More than one Trinity House pilot and Cunard bridge officer has despaired Ocean Terminal III's erection on the *wrong side of the dock*.

It is second *Queen Mary's* beam that most taxes Ocean Dock's efficacy today. At 147 feet (45 meters), she is broader than either *Olympic*-class predecessor as well as the original *Queens*. Despite their deeper drafts, the older liners were slimmer; *Queen Mary* and *Aquitania* could easily berth at the same time along Ocean Dock's opposite sides. The dock's northern (short) end, berth no. 45, remains in freight mode, adapted for loading small container vessels supplying the Channel Islands. Two temporary container cranes belonging to APB (Associated British Ports, the body that operates seventeen UK ports) have been erected pierside.

Southampton's most modern piers are located farther west. Container operations require huge acreage, utterly lacking in Southampton's original dock complex. A forest of container cranes looms over what are called the Western Docks, where there is not only room for those angular, steel praying mantises that can load or unload an entire vessel in a day but sufficient room as well to park unloaded or about-to-be-loaded containers. In fact it is the giant, accumulating clusters of containers that overwhelm much of today's port environs. Since they can be stacked and stored six high, hectares of formerly open spaces have been fenced off by forbidding container walls, effectively isolating and obscuring harbor frontage from the city.

Indeed, all of the port's contemporary visual tapestry is a far cry from 1912. Latter-day refinements have created new longshoremen profiles—hardhats, Day-Glo high-visibility tunics, striped waterproofs, stout Wellington boots, and, always, ubiquitous cell phones. Their industrial surround is no less transformed—chain-link fences, orange/white traffic cones, lorry transporters, huge wind turbine propeller blades, stacks of extruded buoys, brightly colored farm machinery ready for export, and three open-sided, multilevel car garages complete the colorful panorama of today's operation.

Yet regardless of the twenty-first-century context, Ocean Dock's footprint still conforms to the dimensions of that spacious parallelogram excavated a hundred years ago. Its neat margins of granite and cement coping stones and bollards remain a tribute to solid, Edwardian engineering.

Titanic buffs from around the world like to visit Southampton, anxious to glimpse the spot from which their sanctified vessel departed on her maiden crossing to New York. Though she would call at Cherbourg and Queenstown en route, Southampton remains the legend's emotional beginning. But ports and docks, alas, are as impersonal as they are transitory, tied to economic rather than historical perspective. From the moment Ocean Dock ceased accommodating passenger ships, those *Titanic* pilgrimages were effectively vitiated. It is hard to envision that haunting four-funnel profile embarking passengers from a dock muddied with freight.

A hundred years after the fact, history has become just as muddied. Many times have I stood on berth no. 44 and tried to envision that hallowed departure. Given Southampton's present indifference, newcomers have an even harder time. Nowhere in or near the Ocean Dock does plaque or sign hint at its *Titanic* linkage. The only remaining infrastructure of the period is anonymous, cast-iron bollards ranged along berth no. 44's frontage. One of them provided the only *Titanic* souvenir I possess, a rusted, flaking iron shard to which the vessel's bow lines must once have been secured. Though not a fragment of *Titanic* herself, I cherish it nonetheless; long before *Queens*, Union Castle tonnage, or *France* moored there, its initial use had been for *Olympic* in June 1911 and, less than a year later, second-of-the-class *Titanic*.

At noon on 2 April 1912, *Olympic* vacated Ocean Dock to begin a westbound crossing to New York. The day before, *Titanic* sailed from Belfast, her trials completed. Prior to her departure from Northern Ireland, the vessel's two most junior officers, fifth officer Harold Lowe and sixth officer James Moody, were ordered by their chief officer William Murdoch to inspect the vessel's twenty lifeboats. This they did, in company with Roderick Chisholm, the man who had designed them and who would be sailing as part of Harland and Wolff's inspection team to New York.

They checked that each of *Titanic*'s sixteen boats and four collapsible or Berthon boats contained their required equipment—oars, mast, sail, and a canvas bag of rigging. There were, Lowe recalled, one and half sets of oars for each, which they left as was, lashed together with twine. There were also a rudder, tiller, painter, and sea anchor, together with water and bread (hardtack biscuit) breakers. Some of these latter, they reported, were still empty.

Titanic sailed for Southampton the following day. During that evening of 2 April, *Olympic* and *Titanic* could have passed within sight of each other but, if they did, no one mentioned it. By the time *Titanic* had skirted the Brambles and slowed to a stop in the Test's turning ground outside Ocean Dock it was midnight. Since the tide was high and the wind low the vessel could easily be repositioned to enter the dock sternfirst. Shepherded by half a dozen tugs, *Titanic* was turned through 180 degrees in the dark.

There was good reason to do so. The vessel would have to be coaled in the dock during that hectic pre-maiden voyage week. Given the boiler layout—tight-packed rows of five boilers with intervening, transverse coal bunkers—the vessel could be bunkered from either port or starboard. But an additional factor arguing in favor of sternfirst entry was that the working crew alleyway—called Scotland Road after the Liverpool original—favored the vessel's port side resting against the pier. It made sense to turn the vessel at high water on arrival rather than on the pressured morning of departure a week later; with her bow pointing downstream she would be poised for effortless undocking and exit.

Once the liner had been maneuvered into position at berth no. 44, longshoremen dropped her brand-new hawsers over the bollards and secured the vessel alongside. During the hectic week to follow, a token *Titanic* lifeboat drill took place. With Lowe and Moody again in charge, it involved only two starboard-side lifeboats and their crews. Lowered to the water, the crews shucked the falls and rowed a brief circuit around Ocean Dock. Then the boats returned alongside *Titanic*, were reattached to the falls, and hoisted back up into the davits. That solitary drill was *Titanic*'s only one, common practice at the time. No passengers were involved for they would not embark until the morning of 10 April. Lowe's last order of business after his men secured the boats was having them remove their drainage plugs, standard procedure to prevent rainwater accumulation in the bilges.

It is worth jumping ahead for a moment to see how in-port boat drills would change following *Titanic*'s loss. Eddie Burton, a White Star seaman who had served aboard *Adriatic* and *Olympic*, was to have sailed on *Titanic*. But just days before departure, having been granted a long-awaited berth working aboard a gentleman's yacht, he did not sign on. He watched *Titanic*'s departure and was also privy to drills instigated after the disaster, his memory as keen as his syntax was picturesque.

The American Line boats. They was death traps in those days. The *New York*, they'd lower one boat at the end of every trip, always the same boat. After the *Titanic*, they made a new law—'ad to lower *all* the boats and row 'em once around the ship! First time they did that, some of the boats, they 'ad to 'ammer away at the rust and paint on the davits for an hour or more before they could lower them at all, and some of them, the ropes broke under the weight of two men in the boat while it was being lowered, and they all started to leak as soon as they 'it the water.

Coaling *Titanic* would happen that week as well, but getting sufficient coal aboard *Titanic* would prove challenging. Indeed, bunkering any UK vessel in the early spring of 1912 was hampered by a crippling national coal strike that had started on Wednesday, 21 February, and would end seven weeks later on 10 April—*Titanic*'s sailing day, as it happened. But strike's end in no way diminished its impact: the kingdom's coal pipeline—from Welsh mine face to surface, into barges or railway coal wagons and into depleted port bunkers—was empty and resumption of normal supply levels would consume additional weeks.

The strike's effect on Southampton shipping in general and the White Star Line in particular was horrendous. Railway coal consumption was one thing: whereas the locomotive of a boat train between Waterloo and the docks might burn at most only a few tons, *Titanic*'s voracious bunkers required 6,000 tons before each crossing.

Around the turn of the century, Liverpool and Southampton shipping had become the target of rapacious Yankee manipulation. J. P. Morgan had founded what he called the International Mercantile Marine, an ambitious instrument within which the financier hoped to corral every transatlantic hull. He almost succeeded, snapping up the White Star, Red Star, and American lines; the only British holdout was Cunard. Quite rightly, Their Lords of the Admiralty perceived the IMM as a very real threat to Britain's wartime merchant navy. In the event of hostilities, assignment to them of American-owned Cunard would not apply, posing worrisome strategic ramifications.

Morgan's greed did not, could not extend to Britain's restive collieries, however. As the strike wore on, dwindling supplies of Southampton coal reserves put sailing schedules at risk. By the time of *Olympic*'s undocking for New York on 2 April supplies were even tighter. *Titanic*'s maiden voyage, scheduled for eight days later, was in serious jeopardy, despite the fact that *Olympic* had brought eastbound bags of American anthracite stacked in her third class public rooms. Additionally, bargeloads of French coal were towed across the Channel, but this latter was ancient, inferior stuff, much of it with grass growing out of it.

Regardless of that Franco/American replenishment, there was still insufficient coal for *Titanic*'s maiden. So IMM's draconian decision was to order marine superintendents in Southampton to transfer coal from the bunkers of every in-port American and White Star vessel to *Titanic*, enabling her to sail.

In all, five ships were pirated. Moored side by side in the inland corner of Ocean Dock's berth no. 46 were three of them. Farthest inboard lay White Star's *Majestic*, bow inland; tight alongside her was *Philadelphia*, bow out, and then *St. Louis*, bow inland. (The latter had, coincidentally, vacated berth no. 44 on 30 March to make room for inbound *Olympic*.) Farther down the dock peninsula were two more inactive steamers, moored at berth nos. 38 and 39, present-day location of the Queen Elizabeth II terminal, both bows pointing south. Inboard was White Star's *Oceanic*, recently emerged from dry dock, and, outboard, the smaller American Line's *New York*, stranded in Southampton since 12 March.

Securing ships tightly side by side was called rafting and, when ships were rafted, it meant they were not going anywhere and those five were going nowhere because their bunkers had been emptied. Transferring fuel from one steamship to another was a rare contingency. Coal that, gravity impelled, has originally tumbled into coaling ports ranged along the shell plating normally leaves the vessel over time as either smoke or ashes. Retrieving it unburned from the bunkers posed an unusual logistical challenge.

One Southampton historian has suggested that each vessel could have approached *Titanic*'s starboard flank in turn to dump its fuel residue into her coaling ports. But there is no record of their appearing alongside the new arrival and, if they had, someone surely would have photographed the event.

Complicating matters was that the coal to be transferred was positioned so low in the hulls. My sense is that, long before 3 April, each ship had voided its residual coal into barges that would be loaded and ready by the time *Titanic* appeared. But that off-loading procedure was arduous. Coal heavers had somehow to manhandle barrowloads up through the hull from boiler rooms to an upper deck level from which it could be dumped over the side into waiting barges.

How did they do it? First, to off-load their coal, every idled vessel would have to have been temporarily sprung from its rafted confinement. There were no elevators or lifting mechanisms to implement upward shipboard transfer. One possibility might have been to stack coal sacks in the bottom of empty holds so that ship's cranes could hoist them to open deck level. But cranes require steam; had sufficient fuel been retained to power them? However that unique chore was completed, brutal hand labor had to be involved.

Thankfully, since *Olympic*-class vessels' bunkers were sited athwartship rather than flanking the boiler rooms, coal could be loaded into either side of the vessel. *Titanic* did not have to be warped away from the Ocean Dock's eastern side but could be bunkered exclusively through her exposed starboard side. However, it did mean that the new vessel would be repeatedly inundated with coal dust following every delivered bargeload.

When *Titanic* finally departed at noon on 10 April, the combined beams of those rafted vessels in the Ocean Dock's opposite corner were only 183 feet, 10 inches (55 meters) wide; in no way would they hamper her exit. But *Oceanic* and *New York*, rafted farther south at berth nos. 38 and 39, most assuredly would. They were moored exactly where the Test's channel to sea begins narrowing. On the bridge of outbound *Titanic* were the same pilot and master who had manned *Olympic*'s bridge when she had been skewered by HMS *Hawke* the year previous, the bearded pilot George Bowyer and the bearded captain (and commodore) Edward J. Smith.

Ominously, history repeated itself. Proceeding too fast in confined waters, *Titanic* unleashed another hydrodynamic crisis. Her passage en passant sent a water surge flooding against *New York*'s hull, raising it sharply. When it descended, all six lines mooring her across *Oceanic* to the dock parted. She broke free and began drifting toward *Titanic*. *Oceanic* was not immune; her larger hull listed drunkenly to starboard, dislodging a gangway connected to the pier, but her moorings held.

Most of *New York* 's hawsers had been laid across *Oceanic*'s deck and secured to bollards on the pier. One spring line extended beyond *New York*'s after end, looped over a bollard north of the stern.

The pier inboard of the two rafted ships was crowded with pedestrians because, the moment *Titanic* started moving, many who had originally gathered between Ocean Dock berths no. 43 and no. 44 accompanied the vessel south, walking her out, so to speak, a privilege possible because of Southampton's contiguous dock system. Dozens followed *Titanic* past the coaling pier's hook, past *Beacon Grange* at berth no. 40 and, farther south, to berths no. 36 and no. 37, where *Oceanic* and *New York* were rafted. At the moment *Titanic* inadvertently detached *New York* those in the vanguard had already joined others crowded inboard of *Oceanic*.

When those six mooring lines snapped, all but the aftermost spring line parted at the *New York*'s bits. As a result, released lengths of hawser whiplashed violently across *Oceanic* and caromed into the spectators pursuing *Titanic*. Miraculously, only one woman would require medical attention, struck and felled by a flailing hawser.

The after spring line parted at the pier, releasing it in the opposite direction. Hanging down to the water from the vessel's after railing it proved a godsend. Crewmen aboard the tug *Vulcan* secured it to their after bits, helping to retard *New York* 's threatening drift. It was a close thing. No more than inches separated the two vessels at one point. Would that there had been a collision: in that event, *Titanic*'s maiden voyage might have ended with a whimper in Southampton instead of a bang off Cape Race.

The two hulls never touched. Acting on advice from *Titanic*'s third officer Herbert Pitman, stationed with a megaphone on the after docking bridge, Bowyer called for a burst of full ahead power on *Titanic*'s port propeller, initiating a wash of water that stopped *New York*'s seemingly unstoppable drift. Then a second tug managed to get a line on *New York*'s bow and that loose cannon of a steamer was maneuvered southward through the parlously narrow waterway separating moored *Oceanic* from her giant fleetmate, miraculously avoiding steel-on-steel contact with either.

The entire incident was captured on motion picture film, thanks to the presence of an American amateur cinematographer, William Harbeck, and his French mistress Henriette Yvois, who cranked away throughout. But their footage would never, alas, be screened; the undeveloped film, camera, and both cinematographers lie today at the bottom of the Atlantic.

The great irony was that it was Morgan's abortive attempt to corner the steamship market that permitted *Titanic* to sail on schedule. Without the availability of those thousands of tons of coal pirated from stranded IMM vessels, her maiden voyage would have been postponed; had it been, the fatal iceberg encounter would have been avoided. Thanks also to the coal strike, *Titanic* sailed from an eerily silent port; without coal, there was no steam and therefore no whistled salutes.

It always surprises me that *Titanic*'s near miss of *New York*, witnessed by so many on-deck passengers, was never mentioned by stewardess Violet Jessop in her memoirs. She was below deck, coping with newly embarked passengers. The incident must have generated ship's gossip for days to follow but she never acknowledged or referred to it.

Another ancillary departure drama was observed by Lawrence Beesley, the Dulwich School science master traveling second class. He had watched several stokers dash ashore for a final pint just before noon sailing time. As they tried to rejoin *Titanic*, the last of her boat trains was shunted out of its siding, temporarily blocking the men's way. Firemen Jack Podesta and his mate William Nutbean leaped nimbly in front of the locomotive and managed to reembark, but the three Slade brothers had to wait out the train's passing. They were deemed late and refused permission to reboard. Both Podesta and Nutbean survived, as it happened, but that intruding train may have spared the lives of their three drinking companions.

Titanic's cross-Channel passage was delayed by the *New York* incident and she did not arrive in Cherbourg until after dusk. Embarking passengers from Paris, passenger Edith Rosenbaum among them, fretted at the delay as they waited, sitting patiently aboard *Nomadic* and *Traffic*, White Star's two tenders. In the absence of a suitable deepwater dock in the French port, the two were needed for boat-train passengers boarding *Olympic*-class ships that had to lie anchored out in the harbor.

Finally, with her Parisian contingent safely embarked, *Titanic* continued down-Channel overnight and into the Irish Sea before dropping anchor in Queenstown harbor first thing Thursday morning. More tendering: symbolically named *Ireland* and *America* delivered 120 Irish immigrants and dozens of Irish mail bags to *Titanic*'s starboard side where they were loaded aboard. Persistent lace and blackthorn cane sellers accompanied them, and later would have to be shooed off the promenade deck and back onto the tenders.

It was two o'clock in the afternoon before Commodore Smith could raise his starboard anchor and start the maiden voyage to New York. *Titanic* steamed out of Queenstown harbor and past the Old Head of Kinsale. By 5 P.M., passing Fastnet, she vanished beyond our ken.

That night would be followed by three more of a perfectly normal maiden voyage until late in the evening of the Sunday, the fourteenth. Seas were smooth as the ship settled into harness. Westbound passage seemed normal, its only aberration a smoldering fire in one of the forward bunkers, doubtless caused by spontaneous combustion from that damp Gallic coal loaded in Southampton.

Shipboard coal fires were common and not presumed either special or dangerous; no omen was attached to it. Over the years I have sailed, many British fellow passengers have insisted that grandparents, booked aboard *Titanic*, refused to embark because pier-side omens indicated that something about the vessel was not right. Typical of those forebodings was a woman who, as the vessel was about to sail from Queenstown, told anyone who would listen that she had seen "the angel of death" appear mysteriously atop the vessel's fourth funnel; in fact, it was nothing more than the blackened face of a stoker who had climbed up inside to peer over the rim.

There is no more fitting way to close this chapter than to note that on the cloudy, wet afternoon of 24 October 2009 the ashes of deceased *Titanic* survivor Millvina Dean were deposited onto the Ocean Dock waters. Committal of the remains was made from the stern of the harbormaster's tender *Spitfire*, accompanied by *Sentinel*, the harbormaster's boat.

Kate Finnegan organized the ceremony. Millvina's companion for the latter years of her life, Bruno Nordmanis, together with the port chaplain Andrew Huckett, stood ready on *Spitfire*'s stern. As the Reverend Huckett read the service, Nordmanis opened an urn and scattered his friend's ashes. At the same moment, memorial wreaths from the Belfast, Swiss, British, and American *Titanic* societies were cast onto the dock waters. The sun broke through the overcast and the American wreath drifted apart from the others, floating eerily toward the cement margin of berth no. 44, the exact spot where nine-week-old Millvina had been carried aboard *Titanic* by her mother ninety-seven years earlier.

That moving ceremony closed a nearly century-old Ocean Dock circle, commemorating and celebrating the tenacious life of *Titanic*'s last living survivor.

CHAPTER 5

INTO THE BOATS

France *had two classes, first and tourist,*
completely separated from each other.
The only place the two are together is in the lifeboats.

Tage Wandborg, who transformed *France* into *Norway,* 1979–80

The flimsy little thing did not look safe.

Passenger Albert Caldwell describing his *Titanic* lifeboat

You are in danger every time you travel on the sea
for I see you adrift on the ocean in an open boat.
You will lose everything but your life.
You will be saved but others will be lost.

Told by a palm-reading beggar
to *Titanic* passenger Alice Fortune in Cairo, winter 1912

Into the boats—a simple expedient larded with ominous ramifications. Leaving one's vessel in midocean is a thankfully rare contingency, arising after fire, accident, or collision has violated the hull's integrity. A wartime commonality, it is unusual in peace.

Dozens of unseen manifests routinely describe ship's passengers and crew as "souls on board." But only when they take to the boats does the word surface as the coinage of crisis: no longer officers and hands, no longer snobs, serfs, or servants, all become, in extremis, souls.

And for every one of those souls, abandoning *Titanic* was traumatic. Leaving their well-ordered haven, forsaking possessions and exchanging legendary comfort for punishing exposure, was forbidding. Forgotten as if they had never existed were every White Star nicety and perquisite. Shipboard's seductive fabric unraveled, rules and regimes abrogated. The night's only plus was that boats creaked 70 feet (21 meters) down the side to preternaturally calm water; rough seas would have challenged the elderly or infirm coping with small boat turbulence.

Eclipsed by catastrophe, the maiden voyage was over. Rather than wondering with whom they would share a meal and stroll the deck or which library book to borrow, passengers' overriding preoccupation was, suddenly, survival. Whether one departed *Titanic* via lifeboat or shivering breaststroke, the emotional gloves were off: complacency and confusion, dithering and delay had been renounced. Within those twenty lifeboats, some loaded too full, others not full enough, and a few launched capsized, the norm was hardship.

Documenting every facet of the disaster is impossible. Though some of the 1,503, either trapped aboard or hurled into the sea, left gallantly articulated legacies, all would perish swiftly and alone. The 703 who lived to tell about it endured differing ordeals, but of annoyance, discomfort, selfishness, heroism, ingenuity, and, always, bone-chilling cold there was full measure.

Accounts illumining larger truths are compelling, especially in the matter of survivors' gender. Despite the Edwardians' oft-quoted assurance, were women and children first? Survivor numbers do not reflect that priority. Far more crewmen than those assigned to man the boats entered them. (Conversely, due to the absence of any meaningful lifeboat drill, several boats descended to the water carrying insufficient seamen.) Male passengers tended to embark either with permission or exercising privileged clout, but larger numbers of sailors, stokers, and stewards merely stepped nippy.

The overall count of lives lost was appalling. Only a quarter of the immigrant passengers were saved and, of the total crew numbering 907, 685 perished. One subset of souls were women and children. Of the 703 who reached *Carpathia* in toto, 315 were women; by coincidence, the 126 surviving male passengers and 189 crewmen also totaled 315. In all, 52 children and 21 female crew would embark aboard *Carpathia*.

We have already met one male lifeboat occupant, William Sloper, the passenger who cabled such extravagantly fulsome greetings to his father in Hartford. He was a ladies' man and had become smitten on land by a young woman named Alice Fortune, canceling his *Mauretania* crossing in order to sail with her and her family aboard *Titanic*. Once on board, he also made friends with Dorothy Gibson, a New York actress who starred in two-reeler serials. In a 1949 memoir, Sloper suggested that he owed his life to Miss Gibson, her mother, and a traveling companion named Frederick Seward.

Sloper said that he joined the three of them for a bridge game that night at a table a steward set up in the middle of the smoking room, where Captain Smith and his party from the A la Carte restaurant walked past their table. According to Sloper, the parade of notables included not only the master and his hosts the Wideners but also Thomas Andrews, Bruce Ismay, Archibald Butt, and the John Jacob Astors; in other words, a name-dropper's paradise of every VIP on board. Yet if that card table were indeed "in the middle of the smoking room," no party leaving the A la Carte and ascending one deck would have made such a cumbersome detour, looping back aft just to troop past Sloper. I suspect the man just enjoyed positioning himself in prestigious company.

Dorothy Gibson suggested some fresh air before bed, so both she and Sloper returned to their respective cabins for overcoats. At 11:40, as he waited for her to reappear, he felt a lurch as *Titanic* "seemed to keel over slightly to the left." The incident just preceded Dorothy's return and the two of them were out on deck just in time to catch a glimpse of the receding iceberg.

Later, that same bridge foursome walked forward along boat deck's port side, deafened by the roar of escaping steam. Sloper, shouting to be heard, observed that they already seemed to be walking downhill.

Inside the forward lobby, more passengers had gathered, some still in night-clothes, all unsure what they should do. Then Thomas Andrews came "bouncing up the staircase three at a time." Since he was their tablemate, the Gibson ladies knew him but he brushed aside Dorothy's query and continued to the bridge. Shortly after midnight, Andrews became more communicative, confiding to a seventeen-year-old passenger named Jack Thayer and his father that "he did not give the ship much over an hour to live."

The two Gibsons, together with Sloper and Seward, embarked in lifeboat no. 1, farthest forward on the starboard side. The men were encouraged to join the ladies by First Officer Murdoch shouting through a megaphone. Thirty-seven years later, Sloper reproduced his exact words: "Any passenger who would like to do so may get into this lifeboat." Was that scrupulous recall a retroactive attempt to legitimize his departure? Perhaps Sloper owed his life not to the Gibson ladies but the first officer's indulgence.

Lifeboat no. 1 was designed to hold sixty-five but held only nineteen when it reached the water. Ten more would subsequently be transferred from another, overcrowded boat. For those amply dressed early evacuees the cold mattered little. After rowing at one of six oars, Sloper found himself so heated that he happily surrendered his overcoat to Dorothy Gibson.

Contrast Sloper's effortless evacuation with that of immigrant Oscar Palmquist. A Swedish carpenter, he had jumped from *Titanic*'s Boat Deck when it was only "six feet above the surface" with two life jackets lashed about his waist. He plunged into the sea, swimming as fast as possible away from *Titanic* "to avoid the suction."

It was a common fear among those taking to the water, one that would prove, for all swimmers but one, unfounded. Second officer Charles Herbert Lightoller was that dogged exception. In the water, he became entrapped by a different kind of suction, initiated as torrents of seawater poured down submerging *Titanic*'s engine room gratings. The inrush glued him helplessly to their stout steel mesh. Terrifying moments later, a fortuitous blast from below—perhaps an exploding boiler fractured by the incoming deluge—providentially released him.

For the rest, there was no suction. *Titanic*'s final plunge created only a radiating wave that agitated lifeboats far away but drew no one down with her. Ship's baker Charles Joughin, wearing a lifejacket and brimful of purloined whiskey, rode the stern down like an elevator, stepping off at sea level to no ill effect. "I had expected suction of some kind, but felt none. At no time was my head under water."

A hundred yards clear of the vessel, Palmquist heard a loud explosion, *Titanic*'s rupturing death throes. A cabin door was loosed and propelled toward him, which he used as a raft. Paddling to a heavily laden lifeboat, Palmquist reached up and clutched the gunwale. There his fingers were smashed with an oar by a crewman, acting on orders from the quartermaster, who feared additional souls might swamp them, and he had to let go.

But one of the boat's occupants, a fellow Swede, recognized Oscar and took pity on him. She trailed her shawl in the water, providing a comforting link for the swimmer. Palmquist managed to stay if not aboard at least alongside the lifeboat for hours, until it reached *Carpathia*, his hand fairly frozen to that comforting shawl. He was hauled aboard nearly paralyzed; it took days to recover his body warmth.

His savior's compassion proved her mortal undoing, however. Deprived of the shawl's warmth, she succumbed to hypothermia. Palmquist's end thirteen years later was no kinder: he drowned in six feet of water after stumbling into a pond in Yonkers' Beardsley Park.

Another first class male forbidden to enter a lifeboat was Lucian P. Smith. He and his nineteen-year-old bride, Mary Eloise, were returning from a European honeymoon, started months earlier aboard eastbound *Olympic*. Scion of a coal-rich West Virginia family, Lucian had heard about the collision and returned to his cabin where he gently imparted the news about "the boat having a little hole in it downstairs."

He helped his wife dress warmly, advising her to wear a dark suit that would not show the dirt. "He stood there," she recalled, "calmly eating an apple." Then Lucian escorted her up to the boat deck. Moments later, she hastened back to the cabin for a precious ring bought in Paris.

When she returned, Lucian helped secure her life jacket. Captain Smith was standing nearby, and a terrified Mary Eloise begged him to let Lucian join her in the lifeboat. Smith's response, really an announcement cried out to surrounding passengers within earshot, was: "Women and children first!," a sentiment with which Lucian heartily agreed, clapping the master on the back.

"Good boy! Don't think I would ever take a woman's or a child's place."

He assisted Mary Eloise into lifeboat no. 6, kissed her good-bye, and articulated his version of the transparent yet apparently convincing lie told by so many men that night: "I will see you later. I will be there in a minute." Then he stepped back. The last words he called out as the boat creaked down were, "Keep your hands in your pocket so they won't get cold!"

Lucian might have been even more solicitous had he known what his wife suspected: that she was two months pregnant. As it was, he stood at the railing next to Robert Daniel, the Richmond banker who had sent the simpler, shorter Marconigram to his mother.

One of Mary Eloise's fellow occupants of lifeboat no. 6 became its putative commander. She was the indomitable nouveau riche heiress from Denver who would garner later renown as "the unsinkable Molly Brown." They were about a mile from the vessel when it plunged to the bottom.

Lucian's body was never recovered. But Robert Daniel, the fellow American who had been his rail companion, survived despite incredible odds. After the last lifeboats had departed Daniel jumped overboard wearing a flannel nightshirt with his father's watch strung on a ribbon around his neck. The shock of the 28-degree water was fearful and he swam furiously in an attempt to overcome the penetrating chill and, once again, "avoid the suction."

But events from then to *Carpathia* are blurred. One account has him picked up by Margaret "Molly" Brown's lifeboat, in which he consoled a distraught Mary Eloise during the night that followed. Another version has him plucked from the sea near *Carpathia* and brought aboard incoherent with cold and hallucinating. According to ship's surgeon Frank McGee, he appeared to be one of "four dead men."

However he reached *Carpathia*, Robert Daniel revived and, kitted out in one of the doctor's too-small suits, was not slow, as the self-proclaimed "only southern gentleman on board," to devote himself to widowed Mary Eloise Smith's service. Such was her reliance on the man that, when they reached New York, it was Daniel who, almost carrying the newly made widow, delivered her into the arms of her congressman father, James Hughes. He also claimed to reporters, spuriously, that he had helped the two wireless telegraphers transmit survivors' names to *Olympic*.

Three months later, Mary Eloise attended a memorial service for her lost husband in the same church in which she had married him. Family member Taylor Vinson commented, "Mary Eloise was probably the only woman in the world who in just a year's time, made her debut, got engaged, married, survived the *Titanic*, became a widow and then a mother." Two years later, she and Robert Daniel were married in New York's Little Church Around the Corner and young Lucian P. Smith Jr. became part of their household. The marriage ended in divorce after nine years. By then, both husband and wife were hopeless alcoholics, an affliction that would end Mary Eloise's increasingly tortured life in a Cincinnati sanatorium aged forty-six.

Despite his refusal to let Lucian Smith enter the lifeboat, Captain Smith proved curiously selective about other husbands. When Karl Behr, his fiancée, and their friends the Beckwiths reached lifeboat no. 5, Mrs. Beckwith asked Smith if the men could join them. "Why, certainly, madam,'" replied the captain. All four climbed in. Norman Chambers, whose wife, Bertha, was already one of the boat's occupants, jumped into it as crewmen began lowering it to the water.

Many of boat no. 5's occupants seemed curiously detached from reality. They rowed away fully confident of returning for breakfast. Chafing crewmen, reinforcing that belief, bawled after them that they would need special tickets to reembark. After *Titanic* sank, many of those in the boat were convinced that the pitiful cries from the water around them came from steerage passengers only. Moreover, none of them seemed to realize that *Titanic*'s lifeboat count was so scandalously inadequate.

Melodramatics, too, seemed a boat no. 5 specialty. Behr was carrying a revolver. He had been Chambers's classmate at Lawrenceville and whispered into his ear, "Should the worst come to the worst, you can use this revolver for your wife, after my wife and I have finished with it."

Henry Frauenthal, an orthopedic surgeon, also managed to embark aboard lifeboat no. 5 with his wife. He too seems to have been remarkably confused. As they rowed away, he inquired of third officer Herbert Pitman, the boat's commander, what was the exact reason for abandoning ship. Until advised at that moment, he had been completely unaware of *Titanic*'s iceberg encounter.

Other officers besides the master encouraged male passengers to enter boats lacking sufficient women to fill them. Elmer Taylor helped his wife, Juliet, into lifeboat no. 3 on the starboard side. She begged him to join her. By way of response, devout Christian Scientist Taylor recited a familiar Mary Baker Eddy tenet: "Divine love has always met and always will meet every human need."

In fact, Juliet's all too "human need" was answered almost at once. Since the boat was less than half full and no more women appeared in the vicinity, officers invited six nearby men to embark, Taylor included, sparing his wife the infinite desolation of widowhood.

Lawrence Beesley, the Dulwich College science master, profited from the same luck. Fellow male passengers on Boat Deck's port side advised him that, over on the starboard side, men stood a better chance of being allowed into the lifeboats. Boat no. 13 was half filled with women and Beesley heard the loading officer call out, "Any more ladies?"

There were none in sight. Moments later, the same officer addressed him directly: "Any ladies on your deck, sir?"

Looking around him, Beesley replied in the negative.

"Then you'd better jump," he was advised. Gratefully, he did.

Mark Fortune had no such luck. A successful real estate man from Winnipeg, he, his wife, Mary, and four of their six children occupied three adjacent first class cabins along C Deck. The family had completed a winter-long tour including Cairo and Venice. Over Mary Fortune's objection, her husband had packed his heavy buffalo fur coat, a moth-eaten relic he considered a talisman. He relished it against the boat deck's chill that night, perhaps the most warmly dressed passenger on board.

He and his younger son Charles stood next to the lifeboat into which his wife and three girls had embarked. Mary Fortune was carrying her jewelry in a leather pouch. At the last minute, her husband asked her to hand it over to him and he slipped it into his coat's capacious pocket, an apparently successful ruse to convince her that he and Charles would join the family later. They never did, and neither his nor Charles's body, nor the jewelry, was recovered.

Third class passenger Edward Ryan from Tipperary had boarded at Queenstown, sharing a cabin with two other Irishmen who, that night, refused to believe *Titanic* could be at risk. Ryan finally gave up on them.

He climbed up to Boat Deck, knowing it was "barred to third class passengers." Once there, he suddenly realized that he should retrieve his nest egg, £300 hidden in the cabin. But when he tried he found that seawater inundating the lower decks had already rendered his alleyway impassable.

Reemerging up on Boat Deck, Ryan was caught in waves of moiling passengers surging aft. Some steerage women were terrified of lifeboat descent, others refused to leave the vessel without their husbands. As the slope of the deck increased, some desperate men started climbing the after mast's shrouds in an attempt to postpone the inevitable.

Ryan and a third class woman found themselves pinioned by crowds against *Titanic*'s stern railing. Over the side, he spotted a packed lifeboat 30 feet (9 meters) below. He wondered, could he slide down to that boat if he had a rope? Miraculously, he found one, a line hanging over the railing; he hazarded it may have been the vessel's log cable.

Telling the woman that it was only a matter of minutes before they drowned, he said he would wind the rope around himself and she should catch it above him, and together they would shinny down to the boat.

They climbed the railing and, grasping the line, slid down, the palms of their hands immediately abraded and bleeding. But both landed in the boat, Ryan atop a woman whose shins, he realized, his boots had badly skinned. Never mind, they were off sinking *Titanic* and in a boat.

As those at the oars rowed away, they saw the ship rear up and then heard two explosions. Next came that awful, drawn-out noise that Ryan never forgot, fifteen hundred of his fellow souls crying out desperately for help. Perhaps his complacent cabinmates were among them.

Frankie Goldsmith, a nine-year-old English lad, lost his father that night. He and his widowed mother would settle in Detroit near Tiger Stadium. Whenever someone hit a home run and the crowd cheered, Frankie would break out in a cold sweat. His mother realized that the stadium roar replicated that horrifying chorus recalled from mid-Atlantic.

"Then arose," remembered first class passenger Hugh Woolner, "the most fearful and bloodcurdling wail." George Rheims described it as "horrifying, mysterious, supernatural." From atop an overturned collapsible, Jack Thayer compared the sound to "locusts buzzing on a midsummer night, in the woods of Pennsylvania." Although he did not know it at the time, one of those "buzzing locusts" was undoubtedly his father. That extended, searing chorus continued in telling diminuendo for nearly an hour. One shouted plea from among the doomed outcry haunted greaser Walter Hurst to his grave: "Save one *life*!"

Survivors in practically every boat heard those heartbreaking cries. Their inaction and failure to offer assistance borders on criminal indifference, rather similar to masters Stanley Lord's and James Moore's failure to succor *Titanic*. In their defense, rowing and maneuvering the boats was cumbersome and, for those loaded to capacity, embarking additional souls might have proved risky. For whatever reason, almost none of those desperate castaways was rescued.

Lifeboat occupants were not entirely secured against discomfort. All lifeboats have drainage holes that ships' bosuns leave unplugged to prevent rainfall accumulations when fastened in the davits. It was not unusual for crewmen abandoning ship to forget to reseat those plugs. Distraught passengers in many boats, Edward Ryan's included, felt icy water flooding around their ankles. He sacrificed the tail of his shirt, tearing it off and twisting it into a makeshift stopper that helped stem the influx. Fifty-seven years later, when Holland-America's *Prinsendam* burned in the Gulf of Alaska, evacuated passengers discovered that their lifeboats' drainage plugs had also not been reseated.

Spray from mounting seas would have kept *Titanic*'s people wet anyway. Ryan tried lighting his pipe for comfort, but a nearby female passenger objected, reprimanding him loudly, so he put it back in his pocket.

Behavior of this kind was not atypical; class abrasions recurred in many democratically crowded boats. In another, a first class woman, obviously of temperance persuasion, seized a whiskey bottle from a shivering stoker clad in a singlet and hurled it triumphantly overboard; that it might have saved the man's life apparently mattered little.

Throughout almost every boat, passenger antagonism toward crewmen seemed consistent. Although some were assigned to their places in the boats, their presence on board was perceived by the newly bereaved as unwarranted displacement of a lost husband, father, or son.

When Margaretha Frolicher and her mother entered a lifeboat, both women tripped. Later, as they sat along the thwarts, they noticed "about a dozen stokers" lying flat in the bottom of the boat; stepping over them had made them trip. At least one of those interlopers offered compensation. When young Margaretha became seasick an hour later, a stoker with a flask offered her some brandy—the first of her life—and she felt better almost at once.

Second class passenger Mary Hewlett remembered with distaste the crewmen sharing her lifeboat as "mostly men of the unemployed class—and stokers, stewards and cooks—not one real seaman—amongst them were only about twelve women."

Second class passenger Nora Keane, an Irish immigrant, commented on "the horrible people! They must have been fourth class."

Scurrilous or fabricated gossip about the crew was circulated. An unnamed Englishwoman en route to see her sons in the Dakotas grumped to Mahala Douglas, "I was in a boat with five women and fifty men—they had been picked up from the London unemployed to fill out the crew. They would not row, told frightful stories to alarm the women, and when the *Carpathia* was sighted, said: 'We are jolly lucky. No work tonight; nothing to do but smoke and yarn.' Back in London next week with the unemployed."

That gratuitous condemnation was both inaccurate and shortsighted. Branding sailors, stokers, and stewards as arrogant layabouts was nonsense; all of them were just as cold, frightened, and miserable as the unthinking passengers who disparaged them.

Dissension among fellow passengers was commonplace as well. Bertha Watt, who had originally booked a cabin on the idled *New York*, was traveling to America's west coast to meet her father. She overheard a minister in her lifeboat loudly bemoan the loss of fifty years' worth of sermons. Another woman shared with any who would listen her distress about lost jewelry. A newly made widow silenced her with a tearful reproach: "You give me back my husband and I shall buy you jewels."

One understandable and seldom mentioned shortage in *Titanic*'s lifeboats—indeed, in every vessel's—were chamber pots for the women. By way of substitute, an absorbent, rolled-up knitted underskirt was passed from hand to hand in one lifeboat, rinsed in seawater between uses.

Edith Corse Evans was a single New Yorker occupying a comfortable A Deck cabin. Aged thirty-three and single, she and her married cousin Caroline Brown were sailing home to New York in separate accommodations.

Edith did not hear the collision but was roused by her steward after Captain Smith ordered women and children into the boats. Putting on her warmest coat and life jacket she hastened on deck. As she waited, she was alarmed by the deck's angle and confided to her cousin about a London fortune-teller who years earlier had warned her "to beware of water."

By then, lifeboat seats were getting scarce, even for women. Edith and Caroline were actually seated in one boat when they were told to get out and board another on *Titanic*'s other side. They went there only to hear sixth officer Moody call out that collapsible D had room for only one more.

Edith pushed her cousin forward.

"Please, take this lady," she urged. "She has children." Protesting in vain, Caroline stepped in and sat down. Edith heard a crewman suggest that yet another lifeboat might be available and was turning away when Caroline, descending to the water, lost sight of her.

In fact, there was no other boat, and Edith remained somewhere on board, her body never recovered. In Manhattan's Grace Church, a memorial plaque is dedicated to her memory for selflessly renouncing her seat in favor of a woman with children.

Ida Straus was on board with her husband, Isidor, the co-owner of Macy's department store. Hugh Woolner suggested that because of his age, Isidor should be allowed to join his wife in the boat. He refused. "Not before the other men," was his unbending response. When Ida heard that her husband would not enter a lifeboat, she stepped back on deck to stay with him.

I have sometimes wondered where the Straus's awaited their end. Perhaps in their cabin? From Queenstown, she had mailed a postcard to a Mrs. Burkedge in Paris. Part of its message read: "But what a ship! So huge and so magnificent. Our rooms are furnished in the best of taste and most luxuriously and they are really rooms not cabins."

I suspect that the lure of that haven might well have tempted them to remain within it. But Isidor apparently went out on deck at some point, because his body was recovered, while his wife's was not.

Benjamin Guggenheim was sailing ostensibly alone aboard *Titanic*, unaccompanied by his wife, Florette. His Parisian mistress, twenty-five-year-old chanteuse Léontine Ninette Aubart, nearly half his age, was with him but *not* with him, their relationship scrupulously concealed. Each was bunked with a servant chaperone. Guggenheim shared cabin B-52 with his Italian valet, Victor Giglio, while his mistress and her maid Emma Sägesser were accommodated farther along the alleyway in B-35.

Guggenheim and Giglio slept through the collision, and it was Aubart and Emma who woke them up. Steward Henry Etches helped the financier dress warmly and the two men accompanied mistress and her maid up to boat no. 9. Denied lifeboat seats, Guggenheim and his valet returned to their cabin and changed into evening clothes. Resplendent, both men strolled on deck, Guggenheim announcing to everyone within earshot that he was "dressed in his best and prepared to go down like a gentleman," gallantry that became a *Titanic* legend.

Later, aboard *Carpathia*, Irene "Renée" Harris, newly made widow of Broadway impresario Henry Harris, found that she was sharing a cabin with Aubart, whom she described as "a French beauty." Aubart confided to Harris that she had been traveling in company with "an outstanding financier." Fearful of offending his descendants, Renée divulged neither the mistress's identity nor her famous lover's.

Guggenheim had long been estranged from Florette (née Seligman), maintaining a separate household in Paris. While he was dressing "in his best," he gave steward Etches a farewell note for

Florette, who would wait in vain for reassuring news at New York's St. Regis Hotel.

Etches reached New York aboard *Carpathia*. Though obviously privy to Guggenheim's affair, he delivered her dead husband's last words to his widow. "I played the game out straight to the end," Guggenheim dissembled. "No woman shall be left aboard this ship because Ben Guggenheim is a coward." Her husband, his valet, and his chauffeur Pernot all perished while his mistress and her maid survived, the anonymity of their Guggenheim connection successfully concealed for years.

The Philadelphia sisters Martha Eustis Stephenson and Elizabeth Eustis were close friends of the Thayers and Wideners. They had helped each other don life jackets in the cabin and each brought with them extra steamer rugs. The two of them climbed into lifeboat no. 4 through the glassed-in forward end of Promenade Deck's windows, the last portside boat to be lowered.

Hoping for a seat in the same boat was Colonel John Jacob Astor, but a crewman, after admitting Astor's wife and her two female attendants, forbade his entry. Young Madeleine Force Astor, the nineteen-year-old, pregnant second wife of the multimillionaire, hurt her arm as she struggled through *Titanic*'s open glass window at the forward end of Promenade Deck.

Madeleine suffered terribly from seasickness, so much so that she and her husband had not taken their transatlantic honeymoon aboard the Astor yacht *Noma*. They sailed instead from New York on 24 January, booked in an *Olympic* suite. A long Egyptian tour followed before their scheduled return to New York aboard *Titanic*.

That same boat took off all the women on that deck, including the Eustis sisters. But however full of female occupants it was woefully short of crew, with only a quartermaster in charge. Two additional sailors, a bosun and an ordinary seaman, were ordered to clamber down the knotted davit lines to assist him.

Another who would join a lifeboat en route to the water was Canadian first class passenger Major Arthur Peuchen. As he watched boat no. 6 descend, he heard its frightened female occupants shouting up that there were no seamen with them. A skilled yachtsman, the major volunteered to remedy the shortage. The loading officer told him if he were yachtsman enough to climb down the knotted davit line he could do so. Peuchen leaped and grabbed the rope, swarmed down, and was saved, though for the rest of his life he felt compelled to justify his salvation.

Lifeboat no. 4 played host to a large Philadelphia contingent, many in the first class with servants. Mrs. Astor sat between a trained nurse and her maid; Emily Ryserson and her three children were accompanied by a governess and maid; Marian Thayer, Eleanor Widener, and Mrs. William Carter all embarked with maids. They were accommodated together with an assortment of other women from all three classes.

Lifeboat no. 4 was almost unique in that it picked up additional survivors from the water. Three crew who had jumped overboard from *Titanic* were helped aboard, and five more crewmen were later pulled from the sea; one of the latter, it turned out, was Mrs. Cummings's bedroom steward. Although two of that second rescued contingent died, the steamer rugs brought by the Eustis sisters warmed the remainder. One of those three survivors was Paddy Dillon, a soaking wet but voluble Belfast stoker. He had pinched some brandy from one of *Titanic*'s bars and consumed most of it. The half-empty bottle, still in his back pocket, was confiscated and hurled over the side by the quartermaster. Then Dillon was consigned to the bilges, his drunken ranting muffled beneath yet another of the Eustis sisters' useful blankets.

Young Jack Thayer had been sleeping in a cabin adjacent to his parents' and experienced the same slight jar that Sloper had: "If I had had a brimful glass of water in my hand, not a drop would have been spilled." He woke his parents, telling them he was going up on deck "to see the fun." Later, he dressed carefully and sensibly for the cold in a green tweed suit. Then he donned two waistcoats, one beneath his jacket and a mohair one on top. He strapped on his life-jacket before donning his overcoat so that if he wished to shed the latter in the water he would not be prevented from doing so.

On deck, he became separated from his parents but was convinced that both had boarded lifeboat no. 4, unaware that only his mother and her maid had been admitted. Meanwhile, just as Lucian Smith had befriended Daniel at the railing, young Thayer hooked up with a contemporary, Milton Long, in the public rooms.

Near the end, the two stood together out on A Deck, one level below boat deck. It was just after 2 A.M. Hurriedly, they exchanged final messages for their respective families and then watched a forward lifeboat embarking passengers. Purser McElroy, who had helped load it, ordered two dining room stewards who had jumped in to get out. Just before the boat was to be lowered, the chief purser also stepped back out onto the sloping boat deck.

As that boat descended, crewmen handling the forward falls let out the lines too quickly, nearly upending it. Both Thayer and Long shouted to the men at the davits to have a care so as not to dump dozens into the sea.

Then, as water surged aft along boat deck, the two friends shook hands. Long jumped first and Thayer thought that he saw him somehow being drawn back into A Deck; whatever the problem, Long never reached *Carpathia*. Thayer waited until the very last minute before doffing his overcoat, climbing the rail, and sitting on it briefly before jumping away as far as possible into the sea only 12 feet below.

He sank into those numbing depths, swimming frantically underwater—worried about suction—before surfacing, gasping, and shivering, some forty yards from the vessel. When what he described as the second funnel collapsed (it was, in fact, the first), the wash of its impact submerged him again. As he surfaced with one hand raised above his head, he felt the inverted, cork-lined gunwale of overturned collapsible B. The five men who had already taken refuge atop it helped him clamber aboard.

They would later be joined by another twenty swimmers, all men. Only when their capsized craft lost some precious buoyancy, sinking lower until dangerously awash, would they reject the pleas of additional swimmers.

Among those perched precariously on that overturned craft were only four passengers. The balance were all crew, second officer Charles Lightoller together with a band of stokers. Thanks to Jack Thayer's account, this was one of the rare lifeboats in which passenger identities were known. Two Americans were Colonel Archibald Gracie, an independently wealthy military historian, and the aforementioned Thayer, teenage son of that rich Philadelphia family. The two Englishmen were Yorkshire justice of the peace Algernon Barkworth and William Mellers, the only occupant from second rather than first, a middle-class emigrant on his way to the States.

It is interesting too that, in his memoir, Thayer admired his fellow crew castaways far more than passengers accommodated with crew in conventional lifeboats did; perhaps the fragility of their shared conveyance exerted a bonding effect. Though Thayer had first described the stoker survivors as a "grimy, wiry, disheveled, hard-looking lot," he later added that "under the surface, they were brave human beings, with generous and charitable hearts."

One latecomer who climbed aboard collapsible B was *Titanic*'s junior Marconi operator Harold Bride, a fortuitous arrival that, in a way, duplicated Thayer's similarly lucky happenstance.

He and Phillips had been exhausted by their afternoon marathon with the shorted-out wireless. But Bride did manage a few hours' sleep and woke to hear his colleague Morsing conventional traffic. Knowing how tired he must be, he went into the radio room.

Neither operator noticed the 11:40 impact. Bride was about to relieve his chief when Captain Smith came in to announce that *Titanic* had struck an iceberg and a distress call should go out.

There was, initially, some lighthearted banter between the three about which signal to use, conventional CQD or the latest SOS. "Send SOS," was Bride's rejoinder. "It's the new call and it may be your last chance to send it."

But Phillips adhered to CQD and his famous transmission entered the ether at 12:25 A.M., forty-five minutes after the collision, radiating out to surrounding ships. During the nearly two hours that followed, Bride stayed at Phillips's beck and call but never relieved him. Phillips sent him forward to advise Smith that responding *Carpathia* was en route. Returning to the radio shack, Bride saw seamen wrestling with a collapsible and heard the musicians playing "Songe d'Automne."

Phillips remained glued to his wireless, doggedly sending and listening, standing rather than sitting. It was bitterly cold, and Bride went to their cabin to get his partner an overcoat and some boots. He also draped a life jacket over his shoulders.

Bride went forward several more times to brief Smith about approaching *Carpathia*. Near the end, the captain entered the radio shack and dismissed both telegraphers, telling them to fend for themselves. Regardless, Phillips stayed at his post with headset on, despite the seawater now flooding over the sill.

Bride idolized his senior colleague. "He was a brave man," he said. "I learned to love him that night and I suddenly felt for him a great reverence to see him standing there sticking to his work while everybody else was raging about."

Bride went back to their sleeping quarters for the last time to retrieve Phillips's money. When he returned, he saw that a burly stoker had entered the radio room, apparently intent on stealing Phillips's life jacket. Although a much smaller man, Bride saw red and, seizing a makeshift cudgel (what could it have been, lying about the radio room?), brained the intruder from behind, felling him unconscious to the deck. Then and only then did *Titanic*'s telegraphers abandon the space, acting on Captain Smith's orders to save themselves.

They separated almost at once. Phillips ran aft while Bride returned to the collapsible, helping the seamen trying to wrestle it over the side. Suddenly the boat flipped into the sea and Bride, who had been clutching an oarlock, went with it, only to find himself under water as well as beneath the inverted boat. He managed to struggle out and, just like Thayer, was hauled atop the overturned hull.

There was later dissension between Lightoller and Bride—was Phillips briefly among the men huddled on collapsible B or was Bride the only Marconi man present? The probability is that Phillips drowned—his body was never recovered—and that Bride was there alone. Someone had trampled his feet badly, imprisoned as they were between some slats. Bride later confessed that he was too exhausted to ask the offender to get off his feet.

In an effort to raise spirits, Lightoller quizzed Bride in a loud voice from the far end of the craft, asking the Marconi operator to share with his fellow survivors the names of the various ships that had been summoned. Near the end, the entire boatload recited the Lord's Prayer in ragged unison. Lightoller tried desperately to stabilize the overturned craft but, despite his best efforts, precious air kept leaking from beneath it. Soon, all the boat's occupants save injured Bride were standing atop their stricken vessel, which had, by then, become almost completely submerged. Seated and incapacitated Bride could only intermittently gasp for air.

Dawn and *Carpathia* appeared at the same time, but the Cunarder was still some distance away, unlikely to reach them before they foundered. But two nearby boats had spotted collapsible B in the early light and, summoned by the authoritative shrill of Lightoller's whistle, rowed with agonizing slowness to their rescue. Always compassionate boat no. 4 embarked some and boat no. 12 took on the remainder. Seawater brought aboard by the soaking men necessitated continuous bailing. Lightoller presented Mrs. John Black in boat no. 12 with his whistle as a souvenir.

As boat no. 4 was being maneuvered alongside *Carpathia*, Lightoller was astonished to hear a familiar voice from above: "Hello Lights, what are you doing down there?"

It was *Carpathia*'s first officer, Horace Deane, a close friend who had served as his best man.

Young Jack Thayer had clambered, dripping, into boat no. 4 but did not realize it was the one his mother occupied until later. When those two surviving family members were reunited aboard *Carpathia*, Marian Thayer's first agonized question to her son was, "Where is Father?" Jack's tearful response was that he had been convinced both parents had entered lifeboat no. 4. The seventeen-year-old then gulped a proffered tumbler of brandy—the first alcohol he had ever consumed—and slept soundly until noon.

As additional boatloads of freezing survivors came alongside, their occupants were assisted aboard. Children were hauled up in postal bags, their heads protruding, one observer remarked, like kittens in a sack.

One of the first bodies later recovered from the sea was that of John Jacob Astor, heavily ingrained with soot. He had been killed by the toppled no. 1 funnel. As a clearly identified first class passenger, his was the first death certificate filled out aboard the *Mackay Bennett*, one of three cable ships chartered to retrieve the floating dead. The final word of that document typified the brutal abruptness that ended the lives of those hurled into the 28-degree water.

Name of deceased—*John Jacob Astor;* Sex—*M;* Age—*47;* Date of death—*April 15, 1912;* Residence, Street, etc.—*840 Fifth Av., NYC;* Occupation—*Gentleman; Married;* Cause—*Accidental drowning SS Titanic at sea.* Length of illness—*Suddenly.*

There was no preliminary illness, no mortal decline, no terminal anticipation, no friends or family gathered around a deathbed. Of obsequies, there would be none save those organized weeks later. Hundreds of passengers and crew perished in trembling isolation across the surface of that black ocean, remote from those that loved them and those they loved. Lives ended mercilessly: the ones wearing life jackets succumbed to hypothermia, the lungs of those without filled with saltwater.

Titanic's lifeboat ordeal was over. Passengers and crew had behaved predictably—some heroically, others less so. But whatever their demeanor, all were profoundly grateful to have a firm, albeit more crowded, deck underfoot once again, and to drink mugfuls of scalding coffee and cocoa or slugs of restorative brandy. For the rest of their lives, none of those fortunate survivors ever forgot that Phillips's CQD had ensured their salvation from almost certain death.

At midday on 15 May, exactly a month after *Titanic* had gone to the bottom, westbound *Oceanic* encountered collapsible A, riding low in the water with three bodies in it. One was a passenger wearing black tie and a fur-collared overcoat, the other two a stoker and a seaman. When its surviving occupants were taken aboard *Carpathia*, the boat had been set adrift because the Cunarder's davits were full. *Oceanic* crewmen brought shrouds and a Bible for burying the dead, the empty boat was hauled aboard and taken to New York.

Long after *Titanic*'s lifeboats had been emptied, long after *Carpathia* had departed for New York, and long after hundreds of dead had been hauled from the sea for return to Halifax aboard chartered cable ships that obstructive ice field finally relented and scattered in North Atlantic spring weather.

In Great Britain, it is not uncommon for people who complain to be advised: "Worse things happen at sea." In this event, the very worst thing *had* happened at sea. Yet though *Titanic*'s catastrophic loss would resonate for years, the site of the vessel's foundering preserved nothing. The sea's restless surface is indifferent to humans seeking to cross it, retaining no trace of their passage. Those dread killing waters south of Cape Race resumed their anonymity, isolation, and, always, utter unpredictability.

As eery lifeboat coda, I must share a fascinating vignette passed along by fellow New Yorker Winthrop Aldrich about Bruce Ismay, disgraced forever for abandoning *Titanic*. In the late 1950s, a young Royal Naval officer Jeff Hawkins (later Admiral Sir Geoffrey Hawkins) and his wife were staying with friends on Ireland's west coast. One day, they borrowed their host's car for a picnic somewhere to the north. Near lunchtime, in Costelloe, they passed a pair of ruined gateposts, their gates askew. Wondering what the place was, they entered the driveway which delivered them to the remaining foundations of what had once been an obviously imposing manse.

Since the deserted property overlooked the sea, they parked and followed a sloping path down to the cliff's edge where there was a gazebo and a bench. They opened a bottle of wine and ate their sandwiches in that ideal picnicking spot. But as they were finishing lunch, each felt a distinct and unpleasant chill, a kind of ghostly tremor about which both separately remarked.

At dinner that night, their host told them that the house had been Bruce Ismay's final dwelling after *Titanic* foundered. He resigned from White Star, withdrawing from public life into self-imposed exile. And, it was said, almost every day until his death in 1937, he would walk down that path and sit in that same gazebo, staring disconsolately out over the unforgiving North Atlantic.

CHAPTER 6

SURVIVAL SAGAS

Surely oak and threefold brass surrounded his heart who first trusted a frail vessel to the merciless ocean.

Horace, *Odes*, book i, ode iii, line 6

Before writing my first book, The Only Way to Cross, *I had* decided that I would include nothing in it about *Titanic*. My reasoning as follows: the tragedy had been documented so well by so many before me, including of course the eminent historian who was kind enough to write a foreword for the book, Walter Lord. His *A Night to Remember* of 1955 remains preeminent in the field.

However, I made a discovery that some readers may have shared. Glance at one *Titanic* photograph, screen even a bad *Titanic* film, read one of dozens of *Titanic* volumes, or just have a conversation about the doomed vessel; whatever your presumed detachment you will find yourself drawn into the most compelling shipboard drama of all time. As a budding maritime historian, I discovered that I could not *not* include that inescapable transatlantic specter; hence, chapter 3 of *The Only Way to Cross* is called "*Olympic/Titanic*."

When I was doing my research, in the late 1960s, there were many more survivors alive than there are today. Recently, no more than three *Titanic* passengers were still with us, all women and all babes in arms at the time. Whenever they were quizzed by reporters on the anniversary of the sinking, what they recited was what they had absorbed by rote from their parents; none had any firsthand recall about their experiences that terrible night.

The last American survivor was Lillian Gertrud Asplund; aged ninety-nine, she died in 2006. In October of the following year, Barbara West Dainton succumbed at the age of ninety-six. For another year, the sole remaining survivor was Elizabeth Gladys Dean of Southampton, known as Millvina, who was only nine weeks old when *Titanic* sank. But now she too has gone, her life ending in a Hampshire nursing home in 2009, aged ninety-seven.

I interviewed three survivors in depth, two crew and one passenger. The first was quartermaster George Rowe. On the freezing cold night of 14 April 1912, bundled up in his heaviest sweater, bridge coat, and mittens, Quartermaster Rowe was stationed on the starboard side of *Titanic*'s after docking bridge. Twenty minutes before midnight he suddenly saw what he first thought to be a three-masted schooner materialize out of the night and brush past *Titanic*'s starboard side before slipping aft and vanishing.

Rowe remained at his post as *Titanic* was maneuvered fitfully. The engines stopped, were started again, and then stopped forever, leaving the vessel dead in the water. Rowe was neither relieved nor advised about anything. Shortly after midnight, he was astonished to see a lifeboat pull away from *Titanic*'s starboard side.

Then he was finally telephoned and summoned to the bridge. Commodore Smith asked him to bring from an after locker what Rowe described as a box of detonators. They were rockets with which *Titanic*'s master hoped to arouse some response from a mystery ship floating no more than four miles away, Rowe estimated. Smith had tried everything—the ship's whistle, a signal lamp, and wireless—to no avail. Shortly before one o'clock on the morning of 15 April 1912, as a last overt gesture of despair, successive white rockets were sent up from stricken *Titanic*'s bridge. Officer of the watch Joseph Boxhall lit their fuses and those on the bridge and open decks watched them soar into the starlit night. At their apogee they exploded high above, releasing clusters of pyrotechnic stars.

Titanic's rockets were clearly seen aboard that mystery vessel. We know now she was the Leyland Line's *Californian*, a 6,000-ton cargo/passenger vessel. She had sailed from the port of London on 5 April, bound for Boston with a cargo of timber but carrying none of the forty-seven passengers she could have accommodated, only her forty-seven-man crew.

In command was Captain Stanley Lord. Though experienced, he had never before encountered North Atlantic ice. So, at 10 P.M., when he first spied that enormous ice field unnaturally far south, he sensibly stopped his ship to await daylight.

Interestingly, in the aftermath of the tragedy, Captain Lord—who stopped his vessel—found himself cast as the villain of the piece; Captain Smith, who drowned when his imprudently driven vessel foundered, was sanctified as posthumous hero. Despite having received no less than six radioed ice warnings, Smith, since the night was clear, merely posted extra lookouts and pressed on at a ruinous 22½ knots.

The *Californian*'s officer of the watch from 2000 until 2400 hours was third officer Charles Groves. At 11:40 P.M., he saw what he described as "a large liner," brilliantly lit, come out of the east before suddenly stopping. Then many of its lights went out. In fact, the vessel had turned to avoid the iceberg and, in the process, blanked out many deck lights.

Consistently, not one *Californian* officer, when testifying at the British inquiry, ever articulated the name *Titanic*. Instead, they all, as though briefed, embraced disinterested anonymity, identifying the White Star vessel only as "the large liner." Groves remembered later that Captain Lord and he had agreed that the vessel was undoubtedly *Titanic*. Regardless, neither chose to use her name again.

Grove's relief for the midnight to 0400 watch was *Californian*'s second officer Herbert Stone. Sharing his vigil would be young apprentice officer James Gibson. Groves pointed out "the large liner" to both of them before leaving the bridge.

En route to his cabin he stopped by the radio shack. *Californian*'s radio was manned by a single Marconi operator, twenty-year-old Cyril Evans. He could not possibly stay up around the clock and, after sixteen hours on duty, was in his bunk, falling asleep over a magazine. Groves was a familiar and frequent visitor who, intrigued by radio, was teaching himself Morse. He enjoyed listening in whenever Evans let him. That night, he asked if it would be all right and Evans told him to go ahead.

Groves hung up his cap and donned the headphones. There was no sound. He did not realize that to receive a signal he had first to wind and activate what was called the "maggie" or clockwork magnetic detector. Evans, who could easily have shown him how, had either drifted off to sleep or, as Groves suggested in a 1955 letter to Walter Lord, "was laying [*sic*] in his bunk reading."

Had the set been live, even as a rank amateur, Groves would doubtless have recognized CQD, *Titanic*'s distress call. But he heard nothing. Mystified, he took off the headset, left the radio shack, and returned to his cabin. Crucial wireless linkage between the two adjacent vessels had been inadvertently aborted. On such minor trivialities do great events turn.

Later, on *Californian*'s bridge, Stone and Gibson both saw rockets rising over "the large liner." Starting at 0045 hours, five were fired; a sixth was seen some minutes afterward. Their appearance instigated what Walter Lord has suggested is perhaps the most bizarre conversation ever heard on the bridge of a North Atlantic liner. Let me paraphrase.

Gibson: "Look Mr. Stone, what are those lights in the sky?"

Stone (peering through binoculars): "They are rockets."

Gibson: "Rockets? Do you suppose something's the matter?"

Stone: "I don't know. I'll ask the captain."

Captain Lord was asleep on the chart room sofa directly beneath the bridge. By blowing sharply down the connecting voice tube, Stone sounded a whistle near Lord's ear, which woke him at once. Stone explained about the rockets.

"What color rockets?" demanded the master.

It was a sensible question. Well after the invention of wireless, vessels approaching each other at night on the Atlantic would send up what were known as company signals. They were Roman candles, really, color-coded signals that did not identify the vessel but her owning company. The White Star Line's company signals, for example, were two green lights, Cunard's two blue. The French Line's were more elaborate, a nocturnal tricolor: blue at the bow, white at the bridge, and red at the stern; three seamen were mustered to unleash that patriotic salvo. Hence Captain Lord's question to Stone: might the rockets he saw have been company signals?

"I don't know," replied Stone. "To me they appear to be white rockets." As even a child of the period knew, the message conveyed by white rockets at sea meant only one thing, distress.

"Let me know what happens," said Lord. Before hanging up, he advised the bridge officers to go on Morsing the vessel, which Gibson proceeded to do. At the same moment, *Titanic*'s quartermaster Rowe was doing the same with an Aldis lamp from *Titanic*'s bridge. But his signals were never seen aboard *Californian* any more than Gibson's repeated flashes were perceived aboard *Titanic*.

Shortly thereafter Stone handed Gibson the binoculars.

"Have a look at her now. She looks very queer out of the water—her lights look queer."

After examining *Titanic* through the glasses, Gibson agreed that "she had a big side out of the water."

Down in the chart room Lord had gone back to sleep. When the two watch officers said that "the large liner went away at 2:20 A.M.," did they mean she sank or merely resumed her voyage, after an inexplicable two-hour-and-forty-minute midocean pause? Stone sent Gibson down to inform the master. Gibson says he told Captain Lord but Lord disremembered being awoken.

It wasn't until 4:30 in the morning that Lord woke up his wireless operator and told him to go on the air and find out the fate of "the large liner." The moment Evans did so he was able to inform Captain Lord what by then most of the world already knew: *Titanic* had struck an iceberg in the midst of her maiden voyage.

Walter Lord died in 2002 after a long, gallant battle with Parkinson's disease. For years, in the early stages of his affliction, we used to lunch together about once a month, and when two maritime historians get together and one of them is Walter Lord the subject was invariably *Titanic*.

I remember one day Walter, in a kind of whimsical mood, suggested that if there were some sort of time machine or magical means of turning back the clock to revisit history, he would opt not to board *Titanic* but would make a beeline instead for *Californian*'s chart room. Once there, he said he would drag Captain Lord by his booted heels off that sofa, march him to the bridge, and make him maneuver his vessel alongside stricken *Titanic* to take off her people.

Hundreds of lives—*more than a thousand*—might have been saved. But as it was, Captain Stanley Lord did nothing. Throughout the night, *Californian* remained "the ship that stood still," rendering no assistance whatsoever. Though never indicted, Captain Lord was disgraced. He and his son to follow sought in vain to clear his name. In fact, *The Ship That Stood Still* is the disturbing title of a book by another late colleague of mine and Walter's, Leslie

Reade. The author documents Captain Lord's baffling indifference to the stricken White Star liner.

The second survivor I spoke with was a passenger. I knew her as Edith Russell but in April 1912 she was Edith Rosenbaum, an enterprising young New Yorker who was in the rag trade. She was among the 274 passengers who had embarked aboard *Titanic* in Cherbourg, after arriving in the port on the boat train from Paris. She had with her five trunks full of Paris spring fashions. When she got them back to New York, she and her staff would remove the French labels, sew in their own, and sell them as New York spring fashions. Her business sense and taste were impeccable and she had created a thriving business.

Edith Rosenbaum was not alone among her fellow passengers to be confused about events on board following the iceberg collision. *Titanic* was not equipped with a shipboard loudspeaker that would have enabled Commodore Smith to address his ship's company. Even if he had, how to explain the woeful shortage of lifeboats? Only 1,100 seats were available, half the number required.

In the absence of hard information, wild rumors circulated. Women and children gathered on Boat Deck were understandably reluctant to exchange brilliantly lit and apparently undamaged *Titanic* for the chill of a lifeboat. They were encouraged by ship's officers thus: get into the lifeboats now and, tomorrow morning, you can reembark for breakfast.

Another rumor had it that somehow—it was never specified how—damaged *Titanic* was going to be towed to Halifax, many miles away. Lifeboat commanders were also urged to row for the same port to be reunited with their vessel.

Edith Rosenbaum obviously subscribed to that second incredible scenario. She summoned her steward Robert Wareham.

"Wareham, here are the keys to my five trunks. Please take them and, when we get to Halifax, check them through customs and make sure that they go by Railway Express to my address in New York."

Wareham, who'd come from below and seen, firsthand, mail sacks floating on E Deck, responded with uncommon candor: "You kiss those trunks good-bye, Miss Rosenbaum. I've got five little ones in Southampton and I'm worried."

He would not survive. His house, together with many others throughout Southampton, would be plunged into deepest mourning. As one contemporary newspaper reported, "a great hush descended on the town." Entire blocks had upstairs windows draped with sheets, ground floor shades drawn, and garlands of purple crepe suspended from doorknobs.

Utterly distraught, the widow Wareham begged her five children never to go to sea, telling them she could not bear the thought of enduring another familial loss. But the youngest, Cyril, defied her. He joined Cunard as a dining room steward, rose through the ranks, and by 1956 was promoted to manager of *Queen Mary* 's Veranda Grill where I used to know him. His nickname was "Flamer" Wareham because he suzetted crepes with such abandon and so much brandy that he sometimes scorched the ceiling. That was the youngest son of Edith Rosenbaum's cabin steward Robert.

It would be safe to say that Edith Rosenbaum was dressed about as inappropriately as possible for abandoning ship. Inveterate fashionista, she wore a hobble skirt. Gathered at the waist, it flared out stylishly before being gathered again around the knees, the height of fashion for 1912. However elegant, the garment was awkward and confining; just walking was challenging. I am indebted to a fellow passenger from a past voyage who shared with me some doggerel that her mother had taught her.

Come on boys, if you want to flirt,
Here comes a girl in a hobble skirt;
You can kiss her and hug her as much as you please,
You'll never get her skirt up over her knees!

Compounding the felony, Edith was wearing backless, high-heeled, apricot-colored satin pumps. And she carried with her a talisman, a good luck charm that her parents had given her years earlier, after she survived a motoring accident in France that had killed two of the vehicle's passengers. It was a music box in the shape of a small pig, covered with brown and white pony fur. Edith left it to Walter Lord and I have held it in my hand. It was made in Paris and when one turned the pig's tail a music box inside played a maxixe. Edith irritated more than one of her fellow passengers by cranking that music box in their ears.

She left her cabin complete with hobble skirt, overdressed with a smart ermine jacket, a warm coat, and her life jacket, clutching her lucky pig under one arm. With mincing steps, she tottered up to Boat Deck, only to find that for convenience her boat had been lowered to Promenade Deck.

More mincing steps delivered her back down the companionway. Because *Titanic* had a slight list to starboard, the lifeboat hung a yard from the side of the vessel and crewmen had filled the gap with a makeshift bridge of folded deck chairs.

Edith balked. "Wearing this costume, there is no way I can get into that boat!" But a seaman who knew her well seized the pig and hurled it into the lifeboat. One way or the other, Edith Rosenbaum followed it and her life was saved.

The third survivor I spoke with was unquestionably the most endearing. Her name was volunteered by my mother. Knowing that I was in search of survivors, she urged me to find out if Violet Jessop was still alive.

"Who's Violet Jessop?" I inquired.

"She was my stewardess aboard *Majestic* in 1925." We were speaking in 1970 and Mother had remembered the name of her stewardess from forty-five years earlier. Mary and I often find it difficult to remember our steward's name from a couple of cruises back.

"Why do you recall her name?"

"Because I'd had some surgery before that crossing and was not sleeping well. So my charming Irish stewardess Violet occasionally kept me company during the small hours."

The two women talked about their favorite ships, all of them White Star. Both were very partial to *Adriatic* and Violet confessed that, during one winter storm, the vessel had seemed about to capsize. But the part of the conversation that stayed with my mother was when Violet told her she had been aboard *Olympic* when it was struck by the Royal Navy cruiser HMS *Hawke*, then subsequently survived sinking *Titanic* and, during World War I, the sinking of hospital ship *Britannic* after it struck a mine in the Aegean. Violet Jessop had been in harm's way aboard all three *Olympic*-class vessels. One would have thought that fellow crewmen seeing her coming up the gangway would have jumped off the other side, disinclined to sail with that Jonah.

I belonged to an organization called in those days the Titanic Enthusiasts of America; they have since changed the name to Titanic Historical Society. One of the many useful things it did was keep track of survivors. I wrote them in the spring of 1970, asking if they had any information about Violet Jessop. I was told she was living in retirement in the Suffolk village of Great Ashfield and was passed along her address.

I wrote to ask if I could interview her for an ocean liner history I was writing and received a charming response by return post, including driving directions to Great Ashfield. I had my car in London that summer and one wet Sunday morning I descended into darkest Suffolk.

I made the discovery that one dripping Suffolk lane looks just like every other dripping Suffolk lane and soon became almost hopelessly lost. So an additional hour passed before I finally turned down the right dripping lane, at the bottom of which stood

Maythorn, Violet's thatched cottage. Keeping dry under its thatched portico she was anxiously awaiting my arrival.

We were John and Violet immediately and, typically, she blamed my delay on her inadequate directions rather than my stupidity. As she ushered me indoors, I could not help but notice how, despite twenty years' retirement, her stewardess persona had survived intact. Violet still had about her a brisk, no-nonsense vigor that recalled so many Cunard and White Star stewardesses from my childhood crossings.

We sat in her kitchen and, on a very rickety pressure stove she called a Tilley lamp, my hostess set water to boil for tea. I drank more tea that day than I ever have before or since. When I got back to London, I had Harrods send Violet an electric kettle so that she could brew up without endangering herself or Maythorn's thatched roof.

It did not escape my attention that Violet was wearing an auburn wig. I did not find out until I read her memoir that abandoning *Britannic* had done the damage. A mine had struck the port bow and Captain Bartlett was trying desperately to beach his sinking ship upright in shoal water. But as he drove *Britannic* toward the shallows she was already down by the bow and her turning propellers began to emerge above water.

Violet was in a lifeboat down on the water when, to her amazement, all the men in it jumped overboard. Looking aft, she saw why. The boat was being drawn inexorably toward *Britannic*'s rotating propellers. Immediately, she too jumped over the side.

Like most seamen, Violet could not swim. Even wearing her life jacket, she sank like a stone. Struggling to the surface, she came up beneath the abandoned lifeboat, striking her head a punishing blow. She began sinking again, thinking herself a goner. But flailing in the underwater gloom, one of her hands caught hold of another that squeezed back. She grasped that hand and the two of them swam for the surface. Lungs bursting, they broke into glorious fresh air, surrounded by a carnage of broken and bloodied men. The hand that had saved her life belonged to someone she knew, one of *Britannic*'s Royal Army Medical Corps surgeons.

The blow to Violet's head gave her a concussion and for the rest of her life her hair never grew properly. By the time I met her she was quite bald.

While we drank our tea, Violet shared some fascinating information. When Cunarder *Carpathia*, the only vessel that rescued any *Titanic* survivors, was approaching New York, White Star officers on board forbade the crew to talk with reporters on the pier. The company was terrified of liability and did not want wild exaggerations circulated by the press. Every journalist worth his salt in the northeastern United States was waiting at Manhattan's Pier 54 that night, desperate to talk with anyone disembarking from *Carpathia*.

Though some of her *Titanic* shipmates did talk, conscientious Violet did not. The diminutive Irish stewardess fell through the cracks that night and it wasn't until I sat in her Maythorn kitchen that wet Sunday afternoon fifty-eight years later that she ever discussed *Titanic* with anyone. For a maritime historian, finding a *Titanic* survivor who has never been interviewed was a veritable mother lode. Let me share with you some of her stories about that incredible night.

Before I do, however, we must leap ahead. Though Violet appears briefly in *The Only Way to Cross*, she never saw herself in print. Less than a year after our meeting, in May 1971, she died, shortly after breaking her hip in a fall. Her beneficiaries were three nieces, London sisters Mary and Margaret Meehan and Marilyn Skopal in Sydney. Among the pitifully few possessions she left was a manuscript that she had written for a literary competition in the 1930s. She did not win it and her typed manuscript, with which she had periodically tinkered over the years, came intact to her nieces.

James Cameron's *Titanic* film was in production and the Meehans wondered whether Auntie Vi's memoir might have some commercial value. They sent the pages to a small yachting publishing house in Dobbs Ferry, New York, called Sheridan House. Publisher Lothar Simon read it and sent it to Walter Lord for his opinion. Walter read it and, knowing that Violet was a favorite of mine, passed it along to me. I read it overnight and called Lothar the following morning, urging him to take on the book and suggesting, if he and Violet's nieces agreed, that I edit and annotate her memoir.

That is exactly what happened. Once the book was ready, the publisher called it *Titanic Survivor* and it appeared in the shops just as Cameron's *Titanic* film reached the height of its popularity in 1997. Anything with *Titanic* on its cover raced off the shelves; it was the only best seller I have ever had.

What delighted me more than the book's success was Violet's pungent and evocative prose. Her words on the printed page replicated her speaking voice to perfection, the same lilting, slightly Americanized brogue that I remembered so clearly from our only meeting a quarter of a century earlier. Failing any subsequent encounter, reading her memoir served as reunion with a cherished friend.

Violet had been raised in Argentina where her Irish immigrant parents—William and Katherine—had hoped to find their fortune; alas, they realized little but disappointment and death. Two infant sons succumbed to scarlet fever. Violet, the oldest, was struck down with a virulent tubercular illness that left her without the use of one lung. She was actually written off for dead in a Buenos Aires hospital. But she clung to life and her father, who had found employment with the railway, moved his family to the town of Mendoza where, thanks to its clear mountain air, young Violet managed to recuperate.

After William died, his widow Katherine and her four surviving children returned to the UK. While the boys were boarded with an accommodating uncle, Violet's mother signed on as a stewardess with the Royal Mail Line from 1903 until 1908. But increasingly frail health meant renunciation of her demanding shipboard toil so Violet, now the family breadwinner, went to sea in her place, changing her life forever. As a promising student, she might have enjoyed an academic career had not shipboard employment of necessity consigned her to forty-two years of traveling servitude, supporting her mother and three siblings.

Making the best of her disappointment, Violet persevered, thinking of herself less stewardess than seaman. There is a descriptive passage in *Titanic Survivor* that perfectly conveys the tenor of early-twentieth-century crew life aboard her first ship, Royal Mail Line steamer *Orinoco*, moored alongside in Kingston, Jamaica.

> I dressed carefully, that is as carefully as one can, when perspiration exudes from every pore, in a cabin so small that to move suddenly meant disaster to some part of one's anatomy. The sun shone in relentlessly through a tightly screwed down porthole and all the bedlam that coaling a ship entailed was concentrated overhead, to the accompaniment of the ship's winches working cargo, the monotony relieved now and then by the purple language of the stevedores.

Now to *Titanic*. It was Sunday night, 14 April. Violet and her cabinmate, another first class stewardess whom she called Elizabeth in her memoir but whose real name was Ann Turnbull, were retiring. The two women occupied double-decked bunks in a crew cabin below *Titanic*'s waterline. Violet, in the upper, was trying for the second time to decipher a complex Irish prayer that a friend had sent her for the maiden voyage. She was a devout Catholic, but she was exhausted and could make no sense of it. Hoping it would be clearer in the morning, she folded it into her prayerbook, tucked it beneath her pillow, turned off the light, and composed herself for sleep.

Within minutes—at 11:40 P.M.—both women were jarred awake by what Violet described as "a rending, crunching, ripping sound." It lasted eight seconds. How do we know? The gash was estimated at 300 feet (90 meters) and the ship's speed 22½ knots; that makes for a trifle over eight seconds.

Immediately, they heard opening doors and inquiring voices outside in their alleyway. Ann turned on the light and, with massive understatement, blurted out, "Something has happened!" The two young women were reduced to giggles, hilarity that segued into nervous laughter as they dressed hastily, "my fingers all thumbs," recalls Jessop. Both went immediately to their respective cabin sections to ensure that women and children were getting warmly dressed with life jackets secured before hastening up to the Boat Deck.

That task completed, Violet and Ann returned to their cabin and, in a numb simulacrum of daily routine, made up their bunks and tidied the cabin as though preparing for a normal day at sea.

Then came a furious pounding on the door. They opened it to reveal Stanley, an old friend and fellow steward. "My God, don't you realize that this ship will sink? That she has struck an iceberg, that you have to follow the rest upstairs as soon as possible?"

In an effort to chivy the two of them along, Stanley helped choose their wardrobe. Violet was a talented seamstress who made all her clothes. She had stitched a lightweight spring suit, complete with frilly bonnet, to wear in New York. Stanley spied the hat and thrust it at Violet. "Here Jessop, you wear this. Now, Ann, what about you?"

Violet returned the hat to the clothes press. "Stanley, I'm not wearing a hat to a shipwreck!" She kept on her uniform apron, donned her warmest coat, wrapped a scarf around her head, and tied on her life jacket. Then she and Ann left the cabin, closed the door, and started up the nearby companionway. Halfway up Violet stopped with a pang. Whereas there would be seats in a lifeboat for herself and Ann, what about Stanley?

Turning back, she saw him leaning resignedly against her cabin door, watching them ascend. "So long Stan, come up soon yourself, won't you?" Violet called. She never saw him again. "Poor old ugly-faced, good-hearted Stanley," she wrote.

Before climbing to Boat Deck, conscientious Violet returned to her first class section to make sure every cabin was empty. The scene struck her as infinitely surreal, the alleyway brightly lit with open cabin doors revealing beds made and unmade, clothes and shoes scattered on the floor, dressing tables covered with brushes, combs, and jewelry. At the foot of the bed in her last cabin she saw a small eiderdown; thinking one of her passengers might need it, Violet wrapped it around her shoulders. Just as we talk about "my steward or my stewardess," so those accommodating ship's personnel talk about "my passenger," a comforting seagoing symbiosis never encountered ashore.

Then she went to what was called the ship's square, a large space specifically designed for stays in port. Throughout Southampton's sailing day, it had been a madhouse, inundated with last-minute deliveries of books, telegrams, flowers, and chocolates, awash with lost passengers, visiting company officials and cabin stewards in search of ice or missing luggage. But once the port had been cleared and the shell doors dogged shut, that ship's square would remain empty, devoid of use until the vessel reached New York, where it would be inundated with the same turmoil all over again.

As Violet approached its central main staircase, she saw that *Titanic*'s square was not quite deserted. Four men, men she knew well, men normally preoccupied on a maiden voyage, were chatting casually in one corner, still wearing their mess gear. They were Commodore Smith, senior surgeon Dr. William O'Loughlin, chief steward Andrew Latimer, and Thomas Andrews, Harland and Wolff's naval architect, on board as a troubleshooter. Violet had met him the year previous during *Olympic*'s maiden voyage.

All four men recognized the stewardess and waved before resuming their conversation. "They were not taking the seriousness of anything, John," Violet marveled to me.

She started up the main staircase, but her way was impeded by what she described as two "impudent cut-ups," a couple of *Titanic*'s pantry boys. They were climbing the main staircase, each carrying one end of a heavy Gladstone bag filled with gold sovereigns. The purser had removed it from the safe and ordered the lads, "Here, you lot, take this up to the boats and look sharp about it."

Now they were struggling upstairs with their burden, laughing and joking, also "not taking the seriousness of anything." On Boat Deck, as they tried lifting the bag over the raised sill separating indoors from out, one dropped his end and gold sovereigns rolled all over the deck. No one paid the slightest attention.

Out on deck, Violet went to her assigned lifeboat, no. 16, the last one aft on the port side. It had been lowered to deck level and was packed with women. Violet found a seat for herself. Gathered around it on the Boat Deck was a crowd of men, the husbands, fathers, sons, or brothers of the boat's occupants. The two groups were chatting calmly, with seemingly little distress or concern; what was spoken undoubtedly had less import than what was not. The apparently accepted wisdom was that the men would somehow rejoin their womenfolk later.

That civilized tenor was disrupted by the arrival of a steerage woman who had clambered up from the after well deck. She was carrying a baby. Although she spoke a language no one understood, it was clear that she feared for her child's life. Hysterical with grief, she put the baby down on a coil of rope that would shortly be used to lower lifeboat no. 16 to the water and disappeared.

James Moody, *Titanic*'s sixth officer, responsible for loading boats nos. 16 and 14, picked up the infant and, spying Violet among the boat's occupants, called out, "Here, Jessop, take this child." She did so, wrapping it in the quilt she had providentially brought for one of "her passengers"; this was not one of hers but clearly a passenger in need. Keeping the baby wrapped in the quilt, she not only kept it warm but also protected it from the sharp cork blocks of her life jacket. Violet clutched the infant tightly throughout the remainder of that bitter night.

Near dawn, she and her fellow survivors sent up a ragged cheer as they saw a ship, rescue vessel *Carpathia*, weaving through the ice at first light, lofting up blue rockets as she came. She was a midsized Cunarder, launched in 1902. She had sailed from Manhattan's Pier 54 on 11 April, the day after *Titanic* had departed Southampton, carrying 150 passengers for a cruise to the Mediterranean and Holy Land. Down in third class, 565 former immigrants were also on board but only for the crossing.

Like *Californian*, *Carpathia* also carried a single wireless operator, Harold Cottam. At the time of *Titanic*'s first distress call, he was not yet asleep but close to it. Still wearing headphones, he sat on the edge of his bunk and, while leaning over to unlace his boots, heard the electrifying message: "Come quickly, O.M., we are sinking fast. Position 41° 46′ N 50° 14′ W."

Scribbling down the position, Cottam raced forward to the bridge and first officer Horace Deane. The two burst into Captain Arthur Rostron's cabin. Rostron was on his feet instantly. Then he and his navigating officer worked out *Titanic*'s position—58 nautical miles away—and immediately set the Cunarder on a new heading. Only then did he turn and demand of the telegrapher, "Now, Cottam, tell me this all over again!"

Having embarked on a course of action, Rostron pursued it relentlessly. First officer James Bisset said it best: "Like an electric spark, he was hurling around, galvanizing everybody into activity." Even before Cottam had finished repeating his story, the master ordered Deane to summon all department heads to the bridge. His ensuing commands were staccato but wondrously specific, almost as though he had prepared all his life for this emergency.

To the chief engineer: "Chief, I want you to divert all steam from the galley hot presses, cabins, and public rooms and send it to the engines." That night, little *Carpathia*, which had never managed better than 14 knots, was suddenly tearing along at 17.

To the chief steward: "Have your men turn all three dining rooms into hospitals. Send bedroom stewards through empty third class cabins and gather up blankets to warm on the boilers. I want plenty of hot coffee, cocoa, and brandy at both port doors."

To the chief electrician: "Rig electric light clusters at both port door entries."

To the bosun: "Have Jacob's ladders ready at each port door and rig chair hoists as well. Have ash bags or mail sacks ready for children. Break loose the forward well deck cranes and have bosun's chairs ready."

Before dismissing them, Rostron added a final caveat: "Whatever you do, *don't tell the passengers!* I don't want them in the way."

The officers dispersed to wake up their men, and all over sleeping *Carpathia* a hive of surreptitious activity began.

But half of one first class couple was not asleep. Louis and Augusta Ogden were experienced travelers. In a sense, they personified the Edwardians' accepted formula for marital harmony: he rows, she steers. Whereas Louis was a sound sleeper, Augusta was not. She lay awake, distressed by several things. First, that the cabin was intolerably cold without any heat in the radiator. Second, that the sea motion to which she had become accustomed had changed. Third, that her toothbrush, standing in the glass on its shelf above the cabin's sink in the corner, was rattling in a way it never had before. Last, she could hear lifeboat chocks on the deck overhead being broken loose.

She nudged Louis. "What's that noise on deck?"

Grumbled her husband: "Don't worry. Go back to sleep."

Moments later, Augusta heard voices in the alleyway.

"Louis, please open the door and see what's happening."

Ogden struggled into his dressing gown and opened the door. Outside was a steward, as though on sentry duty.

"What's all the noise about?"

"Nothing, sir. Doing work on the boats."

"What for?"

"I can't tell you, sir."

Louis closed the door and reported back to the war department. The noise continued.

"Try again," Augusta suggested.

When Louis opened the door a second time, he encountered the ship's senior surgeon Frank McGee.

"Doctor, what's the trouble?"

"There's no trouble. Please stay inside your cabin. Captain's orders."

After Louis closed the door, Augusta insisted, "Ask him again."

This time, McGee confessed. "We are going to the *Titanic*. She's in distress." A line of stewards carrying blankets hurried past.

For no good reason, Ogden was convinced that *Carpathia* was on fire. "But is *this* ship in distress?"

"No sir, it's the *Titanic*. She's struck ice."

Louis and Augusta dressed hurriedly and slipped out on deck. Louis found a quartermaster he had befriended earlier in the voyage who confided, "There has been an accident to *Titanic*."

"That's on the northern route, we're on the southern," countered Ogden.

"We're going north like hell! Now please, you must get back to your cabin."

Evading him, both Ogdens remained on deck. Within twenty minutes the entire ship knew. Gossip is the inescapable currency of shipboard. They used to say aboard first *Queen Elizabeth* that if you stood on the bow and whispered a secret into someone's ear and immediately ran to the stern, the moment you got there you would hear that same secret embellished. All over *Carpathia*, knots of passengers gathered; some wore overcoats over their dressing gowns, some were fully dressed. They all kept out of the way.

We have another *Carpathia* witness of that unforgettable night. Rostron knew he was entering ice and posted additional lookouts. Since first officer James "Billy" Bisset had the sharpest eyes on board, Rostron posted him at the far end of the starboard bridge wing, away from any light source. In one of his three admirable volumes of memoirs, Bisset recounts how he stood out in the cold, exiled from the wheelhouse. Looking back, thanks to the binnacle's faint glow, he could just make out Captain Rostron in silhouette, holding the visor of his cap an inch or two above his head. His eyes were closed and his lips moving. An intensely devout man, Rostron was asking God's blessing on his errand of mercy.

A second incident that Bisset remembered clearly was peering into the night and seeing a pinprick of light directly ahead. Wondering what it was, he decided it warranted a course change.

"Hard astarboard!" he bellowed to the helmsman. *Carpathia* swung to port in a crash turn, skirting past a towering wall of black ice. What Bisset had seen was the reflection of a single star in its surface, which leads us to believe that had Frederick Fleet and Reginald Lee in *Titanic*'s crow's nest shared Bisset's vigilance, there might well have been no collision.

Bisset was not the only occupant of a bridge wing. Rostron had posted a seaman on the port side who, every fifteen minutes, sent up company signals, two blue lights, into the night.

The rising sun tinged the ice pink and orange and revealed *Titanic*'s lifeboats spread across an expanse of floating debris. Paneling, doors, mattresses, pillows, and coffee beans came gouting up from the wreck. Captain Rostron maneuvered *Carpathia* carefully, making a lee against the freshening breeze as, one by one, the boats came alongside, some dangerously overloaded, others scandalously underloaded, some capsized with survivors perched on overturned hulls.

Those passengers who could struggled up Jacob's ladders suspended from the port doors; those who couldn't were hoisted up in bosun's chairs. Children were brought on board bundled into mail sacks or ash bags. Violet, clutching the now crying baby, was taken up in a bosun's chair and deposited on *Carpathia*'s forward well deck. Crewmen had to help unfold her arms, which had become locked in place throughout those icy hours of protective embrace. But as the child was taken from her its mother, who had reached *Carpathia* in another boat, seized her baby. Never once during the days that followed did she attempt, even in dumb show, to thank the stewardess who had saved her child's life. We'll hear more from that baby later.

On one of many trips between the bridge and the port doors, Rostron spied Louis Ogden leaning over the Promenade Deck railing. The captain urged him to get his new camera and take some photographs. He retrieved it from his cabin and took memorable views of *Titanic*'s boats. He recalled how quiet it was, the only sound water lapping *Carpathia*'s stationary hull, the muted voices of crewmen maneuvering the boats, and the sound of a baby crying, doubtless Jessop's charge. Mrs. Ogden joined him and suggested that the boatloads of survivors seemed somehow festive, dressed as though for a summer garden party; of course, it was the white of their life jackets.

Californian appeared. Captain Lord asked Rostron if there was anything he could do. *Carpathia's* master told him to search for additional survivors. Before leaving the site, he spoke at a brief memorial service in the main lounge. Then he turned his ship back toward New York.

Over the following days and nights, the two Harolds—Harold Cottam and Harold Bride, *Titanic*'s surviving Marconi operator—manned *Carpathia*'s telegraph key day and night, tapping out the names of passengers on board; perhaps predictably, the names of surviving crew members were not transmitted. The Cunarder's radio could not reach either shore but her signals were picked up by eastbound *Olympic* whose more powerful set could reach both England and America. Because of that double transmission, names were garbled or lost, and when *Carpathia* sailed into New York on the evening of 18 April no one knew for sure who had been saved and who had not. It would be safe to say that of all the ocean liners that have ever entered the port, none was more anxiously awaited than little *Carpathia* that night of 18 April 1912.

As she steamed into the upper bay, a raging thunderstorm soaked ten thousand New Yorkers lining the Battery. Press boats materialized out of the rain to either side of the inbound Cunarder. Reporters on board rolled newspapers into megaphones, yelling at survivors to put a note into a bottle. "Jump overboard," they bawled. "We'll save you!"

After *Carpathia* had anchored briefly at quarantine, Rostron weighed anchor and took his vessel up the North River, steaming past Cunard's Pier 54 and continuing farther north to White Star's Chelsea piers. Few of the thousands watching from shore realized what he was up to. As it was, with six *Titanic* lifeboats stacked on the bow, mooring the vessel would be impossible. Only after they had been lowered to the water and rowed ashore by White Star crewmen could Rostron turn *Carpathia* back downstream, bring her alongside the north side of Pier 54, and tie up.

Waiting with feverish impatience inside Pier 54's shed were hundreds of relatives of *Titanic*'s passengers, desperate to greet the survivors. The first person down the gangway was a crewman in yellow oilskins; a great groan of disappointment went up. Next appeared a couple too smartly dressed to be survivors; they were *Carpathia* passengers who, given an extra night in New York, were hurrying to see a Broadway show.

But the next person at the head of the gangway was a woman clad in an ermine jacket and a long skirt made from a *Carpathia* steamer rug, the veritable motley of shipwreck. Her appearance elicited a shriek and a woman rushed forward to embrace her sister. As other survivors came ashore one by one, there were more tearfully joyous reunions. But after all 703 survivors had negotiated that gangway, hundreds more of those waiting realized that their vigil was in vain: their family members must be dead.

One survivor had an overdue reservation at the Plaza Hotel. He was greeted at the front desk by the manager and asked if there was anything he needed. More than anything, the man said, he would like a toothbrush; he had been unable to brush his teeth for three days. The manager found one and the man retired, exhausted, to bed.

Music haunts *Titanic* because of what one can only describe as her eight gallant bandsmen who played under the direction of violinist Wallace Hartley. They had embarked as two autonomous musical groups, a piano trio that played exclusively outside the A la Carte restaurant and a piano quintet that provided music in the reception room outside the main restaurant before lunch and dinner. Occasionally, that larger string ensemble would play for second class as well.

They never performed together save after the collision. At Captain Smith's suggestion, purser Hugh McElroy mustered them in the main lounge as a single musical unit. One of two pianists dropped out, which left intact a piano septet. Later, they played at the top of the main staircase where there was a piano chained to the bulkhead. Clad in overcoats and life jackets, it was apparent that they had been temporarily dismissed to return to their E Deck quarters for warm clothing.

Later, we find them playing out on Boat Deck's port side forward where there was no piano; the other pianist also dropped out. Knowing ship's musicians as I do they doubtless stayed nearby.

Serenading passengers in the cold was not easy. Catgut does not perform well at low temperatures and violinists discovered that the cork blocks of their life jackets made it difficult to tuck instruments beneath their chins. I once asked a cellist if he could play standing up and, after a few measures, he described it as intensely uncomfortable. There were no chairs or music stands and inadequate lighting so they played, perforce, only familiar tunes by heart.

People on both shores were anxious to find out the last tune *Titanic*'s musicians were playing before the deck canted so badly beneath their feet that they abandoned their instruments. Everyone wanted it to be a hymn; "Nearer, My God, to Thee" was the favored choice. But the hymn boasts two tunes, one English and one American, and no one was quite sure that they had actually heard either.

Harold Bride, *Titanic*'s surviving wireless operator, provided a tantalizing clue. He had spent much of that bitter night atop an overturned lifeboat. His feet had been badly injured. Doctors warned him that amputation could not be avoided. With both legs heavily bandaged, he was one of the last to come down *Carpathia*'s gangway, pushed in a wheelchair by two attendants from Saint Vincent's Hospital.

Ship's reporters always knew the Marconi men and, as Bride was heading toward a waiting ambulance, one shouted, "Bride, what was the band playing?"

The injured telegrapher turned and, before entering the ambulance, shouted over his shoulder, "They were playing 'Autumn.'"

The hymnologists raced back to their hymnals and unearthed a hymn tune called "Autumn," the third stanza of which features the line *Oh Lord, hold my head up in mighty waters*. So hymn tune "Autumn" became the front-runner in the last-tune sweepstakes.

Nearly three decades after publishing *A Night to Remember*, Walter Lord completed his last book, a sequel called *The Night Lives On*. In it, he wanted to clear up some loose ends about *Titanic*, among them the public's fixation on "Autumn." We don't know hymns by the names of their tunes, he pointed out, only by their first lines. For instance, although none of his readers might be familiar with a hymn tune called "Saint Gertrude," it is in fact the music accompanying "Onward Christian Soldiers."

So Walter searched hundreds of 1911 and 1912 song sheets for another "Autumn" reference and found one. It was a bittersweet waltz, written by the Englishman Archibald Joyce. Symptomatic of contemporary Edwardian pretension, he had given it a French name: "Songe d'Automne," thought or dream of autumn, which Harold Bride had simply abbreviated to *Autumn*. The tune was a hit in London and New York so it was repeatedly requested aboard every ship connecting them.

None of Wallace Hartley's eight musicians survived. One passenger remembers near the end seeing their instruments abandoned, obvious indication of the musicians' desperation.

When Hartley's body was recovered from the sea by the cable ship *Mackay Bennett* out of Halifax, there was a music case strapped across his chest. One wonders, was it music he had hoped to play that night or just music he was anxious to save? At his funeral in his hometown of Colne in Lancashire, no less than six brass bands played in the cortege following the coffin.

Three more items should be addressed. In 1898, an American novelist named Morgan Robertson had published a book he called *Futility*. It was the story of the world's largest liner that sailed from Liverpool to New York on its maiden voyage. In midocean, she struck an iceberg and went to the bottom with huge loss of life. That consumed the author's first chapter. In chapter two, the vessel's survivors discover that there are Eskimos living on the berg and the plot goes crazy. Most intriguing is the name that the author chose for his mythic liner: *Titan*. It lacked only the final White Star suffix *-ic*. His volume was published fourteen years before *Titanic* sailed.

Violet Jessop told me that a fortnight before I showed up at her house the telephone had rung in the middle of the night. There was a thunderstorm miles away and often, when lightning struck the line, her telephone jangled. But she awoke to hear that the telephone was actually ringing. In those days, the English always kept their telephones in the hall, never in the bedroom, the kitchen, or the sitting room.

Violet staggered into the hall and lifted the receiver. A woman's voice asked, "Is this Violet Jessop, who was a stewardess aboard *Titanic*?"

"Yes, it is. Who is this?"

The woman ignored her. "Is this the Violet Jessop who saved a baby that night?"

"Yes it is. Who are you and why are you calling at this hour?"

The caller laughed and said, "I was that baby," and then hung up.

I suggested to Violet that it must have been village children playing a joke on her but she insisted I was mistaken. "No one in the village knows that story about the baby. You are the only person I've ever told it to."

So we're left with an incredible mystery. If it really was the baby grown up, how had she tracked down Violet living in retirement? And why call in the middle of the night? Was she telephoning from the States, not realizing the time difference? Why not visit Violet at Maythorn and have a proper reunion? Whatever the case, she never called back or communicated again.

A fellow passenger of mine once suggested that perhaps Violet may only have dreamed about that telephone call. But I am convinced she still had all her marbles; I think she had some of mine as well.

The last thing I share with you is really nothing but, at the same time, it is everything. Harold Phillimore was a bath steward aboard *Titanic* who found himself in the water that night with no life jacket. He managed to stay afloat only by clutching a bundle of deck chairs lashed together with twine. That had been the inspired work of Thomas Andrews and the chief deck steward, who had filled their final hours assembling those invaluable flotation devices and hurling them over the side. Though both men lost their lives, others were saved by their industrious foresight.

Phillimore, his teeth chattering and lips blue with cold, saw an Englishman, wearing a life jacket and dressed in black tie, paddling feebly toward him. When he clutched the other side of the floating deck chairs, the two men trod water only two feet apart, face to face. Phillimore did not know him nor did the Englishman know Phillimore. They were just two survivors hanging on for dear life in that brutally cold Atlantic.

Phillimore recalled that the man stared up at the great dome of stars covering the night sky. Then he turned toward upended *Titanic*. It looked, as Edith Rosenbaum had suggested, "like the Flatiron Building," a real New Yorker's image. From over the intervening waters came the heartbreaking cries of more than a thousand of their fellow souls, shrieking, freezing, and dying as they were hurled into the sea.

The Englishman turned back to Phillimore and, awestruck, muttered, almost to himself, "What a night! What a night!" Then, in extremis, he relinquished his hold on the deck chairs and drifted away. They were doubtless the last words he ever spoke.

What a night; what a night, indeed. Thank you for sharing it with me.

CHAPTER 7

"SAFE CARPATHIA"

I can't handle her very well.
We have women and children and only one seaman.

Fourth officer Joseph Boxhall's plea from the first *Titanic* lifeboat

When Boxhall boarded, Rostron took him aside.
"I put that heart-rending inquiry, knowing with a terrible certainty what his answer was to be. The Titanic *has gone down? 'Yes,' he said; one word that meant so much—so much that the man's voice broke on it. "She was hoodoo'd from the beginning . . .'"*

Captain Arthur Rostron, master of *Carpathia*

Carpathia *was a 13,603-ton workaday Cunarder, built at* Wallsend by Swan Hunter, Whigham Richardson. Entering service in 1903, she was 540 feet (164 meters) overall, 64 feet (19 meters) in the beam with a single stack, four masts, and twin screws driven by reciprocating engines. The vessel alternated between the immigrant run from Fiume and Naples to New York or, upgraded for transatlantic service, sailing out of Liverpool with 100 first class, 200 second class, and an astonishing 2,250 in third; that so many could be embarked within such a modest hull betrays the notorious crowding immigrants of the period endured.

The vessel had five passenger levels, in descending order: promenade, saloon, shelter, upper, and main decks. First class passengers were accommodated on promenade and saloon decks at the vessel's pinnacle, with dining saloon, lounge, smoking room, and library within convenient reach.

Second class was restricted to shelter deck with a dining saloon overlooking the bow and open deckspace aft. Third class passengers were housed on the forward ends of the two lowest decks, sleeping in a dense mass of individual cabins forward on main deck, ascending one deck higher for meals and primitive sanitary facilities. The after-halves of both third class decks were given over to crew quarters, engine spaces, and provision lockers.

Although she was in some ways crowded, the flip side was that every element of first class country was handily adjacent, indoors and out. Passengers in deck chair or smoking room needing something from their cabins required only the briefest excursion. First class's privileged enclave seemed like a self-contained yacht perched atop the vessel. *Carpathia* was scarcely suited, as we shall see, to suddenly doubling her passenger load in midocean.

All that lay ahead when, at noon on 11 April 1912, the vessel sailed from New York for a spring cruise to the Mediterranean. One hundred and twenty had booked in first and another fifty in second; suiting Cunard's cruising demographics, first and second were consolidated within one democratic class.

Lower-deck occupants were segregated by more than class barriers. The 565 passengers accommodated in third class were former Slavic or Italian immigrants sailing home to visit relatives, identified throughout the shipping industry as "old home traffic." Thus did two disparate passenger groups share the same hull. Whatever languid port calls their upscale shipmates anticipated, *Carpathia*'s humbler clientele were aboard only for a crossing.

Manned by three hundred in crew, there were 1,035 souls (passengers and crew combined) aboard. Still, more than half *Carpathia*'s lower-deck cabins were unoccupied. The little Cunarder could have accommodated almost the same number she was carrying again.

Befitting every cruise, *Carpathia*'s passenger mind-set differed markedly from that of the vessel's habitual occupants. Rather than remaining on board just for a crossing, *Carpathia*'s cruising contingent would occupy the vessel for weeks. First landfall would be

Gibraltar, a familiar sight to P&O and Orient Line clienteles but unfamiliar to most of *Carpathia*'s 170 Americans. Few had sailed the southern route to the Mediterranean and expectations ran high; the legendary rock would herald a Baedeker's worth of antiquity-rich calls, climaxed by the Holy Land.

The mood on board was contented, largely because landfall anxiety did not exist. Every crossings's twin goads—speed and arrival time—mattered little. These were not passengers who would disappear once their vessel touched Europe, not businessmen with a tight-packed schedule, not families girding for a round-robin of capitals, cathedrals, châteaus, and palaces. They were largely retirees enjoying a languid passage that had no other purpose than their pleasure, amusement, and education.

Not all were retired: the Howard Chapins of Providence were honeymooning and Macy's wine buyer was on his way to Portugal to sample the latest vintages. One prominent item of deck cargo lashed to a forward railing was a crated Packard; though its stenciled destination read *Genoa*, the vehicle would actually be offloaded in Naples. It belonged to the three Fowler sisters, Baltimoreans who planned a postcruise continental motor tour. They had engaged Laurence Stoudenmire, a bright young student at the Baltimore Polytechnic Institute, as their chauffeur. Stoudenmire, a keen photographer and diarist, was thrilled to be on his first crossing.

So too was a young couple from St. Louis, Carlos and Katherine Hurd, aboard for a long-anticipated holiday. Occupying a tourist class cabin aft, they ate at a large table, surprised and delighted with everything they encountered. Hurd was a crack young reporter for the *St. Louis Post-Dispatch* and it is one of the curious happenstances of maritime history that on 10 April, the day before embarkation, Hurd had visited the office of the *New York World*, the paper with America's largest circulation. In addition to touring the paper's impressive plant, he introduced himself to a long-admired idol, legendary city editor Charles Chapin. Always busy, Chapin had little time for out-of-town visitors but, thanks to every newsman's inbred fact-retention, he would remember Hurd's presence aboard *Carpathia*. The significance of their brief meeting would resonate in the days to come. Another journalistic colleague on board was Colin Cooper, who created illustrations for the *New York Tribune*.

Pleasurable detachment was the order of those first sea days as passengers relished their shipboard idleness. Deck chair, smoking room, and dining saloon chat between newmade friends dwelt on intriguing destinations ahead. Seas were calm, the sun shone, the Gulf Stream was already offsetting New York's April chill, and the prospect of extensive onboard tenancy had already cemented congenial ties with cabin and dining staff. Steward Robert Vaughan liked cruises because things did not disappear from his shared cabin the way they had aboard crossing *Mauretania*; for some obscure reason, he reckoned that cruising reduced crew-country pilferage.

Mr. and Mrs. Louis Ogden from New York's Tuxedo Park, whom we met in the last chapter, were staunch Cunard repeaters, and as such, were assigned seats at the captain's table. Inveterate travelers, the couple were familiar with many ships. At their first dinner, Ogden told the master about the new Zeiss camera they had bought in anticipation of touring the Holy Land. Mustachioed and sporting a flat cap, white shoes, and three-button tweed suit, Ogden was a gregarious, upper-class American. Daily, he roamed *Carpathia*'s decks, as he did every vessel on which he sailed, introducing himself impulsively to crew members of every rank.

As the vessel plodded toward Gibraltar, officer of the watch James Bisset was chatting with Captain Rostron. (Both men would ultimately be knighted and serve as commodores of the Cunard Line.) Born in 1869, Rostron was a Lancashire lad who, aged fifteen, had sailed on square-riggers 'round the Horn, a brutal maritime baptism that nevertheless fostered a lifelong love of the sea. Tough as oak, Rostron could use his fists if necessary yet remained largely quiet and introspective; not fond of drink, he stayed contentedly on board while shipmates caroused ashore. Rostron would describe a faithful churchgoer in his memoirs: "He doesn't have to boast about his beliefs but is not ashamed of them."

For seventeen years he had served on a variety of Cunard vessels. Slated for a junior officer's berth aboard *Lusitania,* he was appointed instead master of the Cunard cargo vessel *Brescia*. *Carpathia* was his first passenger command. He had been captain for only three months, adequate time for subordinates to absorb and respect his brisk and appealing persona.

Rostron was a natural, archetypal Cunard captain. He looked the part, wearing his cap at a jaunty, starboard slope and favoring tall stick-up collars cradling a neatly tied tie. He was bone thin, with sharp features; though forbiddingly knowledgeable, he often boasted a twinkle in his eye. Postwar master of *Mauretania,* he brought her into Southampton on such a consistent transatlantic schedule that he could regularly board the 3:15 P.M. train home to Liverpool.

Some years later he was appointed Cunard's commodore aboard *Berengaria*. American adolescent Anna Glen Butler once embarked with her family, leading a beloved dog on a leash. When advised that her pet had to be delivered to the ship's kennel, she asked a nearby crewman to take care of the matter; with a punctilious bow and quiet smile Commodore Rostron obliged.

It has always struck me how similarly driven were two pivotal *Titanic* players, *Carpathia*'s master and the wireless inventor Guglielmo Marconi. Rostron seemed just as determined and preoccupied with every one of his burdensome day-to-day challenges, and shared the same characteristics and obsessive preoccupation as the Italian genius. Though obviously not in pursuit of wireless perfection, he was just as dedicated to irreproachable, almost superhuman standards of seamanship. Rostron's admirable handling of *Titanic*'s catastrophe adhered to a kind of textbook perfection, as though the man instinctively knew precisely what should be done.

Bisset was not impressed with the whole idea of wireless. *Carpathia*'s set had a daytime range of only 150 miles. Equally damning was Bisset's evaluation of Marconi telegrapher Harold Cottam. "We considered him," he would write, "to be of very little use." A traditionalist, Bisset felt that a bridge officer's view, eight miles to the surrounding horizon, was a more than adequate means of avoiding oncoming vessels or objects.

During their third midocean morning, as *Carpathia*'s steady 14 knots churned out her daily 336 nautical miles, neither Rostron nor Bisset, nor indeed any of the ship's company, had the faintest inkling that within twenty-six hours *Titanic*'s urgent distress call would be picked up by the disparaged Cottam in the nick of time, summoning the Cunarder to her assistance.

The evening of the fourteenth was typically peaceful. Bisset's watch, the eight to twelve, was the most sociable because it more nearly approximated his colleagues' waking hours; fellow officers repeatedly passed through the bridge. Once again, Rostron and Bisset were chatting about the obstructive ice field to the north; its intruding chill was already tainting the newfound Gulf Stream warmth. Both men wondered how it would affect *Titanic*, whether she would have to divert south and lose time. Rostron spoke feelingly about Commodore Smith, and about how an ice delay might condemn new *Titanic* as a "slowcoach" on her maiden crossing.

Bisset had peripheral knowledge denied Rostron, because he had visited *Olympic* three days earlier in New York. He tramped back down to Pier 54 unimpressed, branding her a steamer "too big to handle." Or might Bisset's negative appraisal have been judicious retrospection when writing his memoirs four decades later? He felt critical not only of *Olympic*'s size but also of her lack of doubled lateral hull and the inadequate height of her watertight compartmentation. But had he in fact absorbed those shortcomings during a brief shipboard tour? I think not. He also condemned as "tragic optimism" *Olympic*'s boast of unsinkability. But "unsinkable" was never *Olympic*'s catchphrase, it was *Titanic*'s. Which leads one to believe that memoirist Bisset may well have been Monday-morning quarterbacking.

Rostron retired at ten and, two hours later, Bisset was relieved by first officer Deane. He went to bed himself, having already noted in the log that by 11 P.M. all of *Carpathia*'s on-deck lights and public room illumination had been extinguished, a common practice on small ships with a mostly elderly passenger load. The only burning on-deck light glowed from the radio shack windows where Cottam was still sparking away, dispatching what little traffic there was. Passengers felt little need to communicate with home at the start of a long cruise.

Earlier that day, when Cottam's steward Vaughan had proposed cleaning his combined cabin and radio shack, Cottam had put him off. He wanted an afternoon siesta because he was planning a late-night wireless vigil, hoping, among other things, to find out more about the aftermath of Britain's coal strike.

Near twelve-thirty in the morning, Cottam called up *Titanic* to inquire about some routine traffic awaiting the White Star vessel from MCC, Marconi's Cape Cod station. That was to have marked the end of his wireless duties before retiring. But, famously, Cottam, at twenty-five minutes past midnight, still wearing his headphones and sitting on the edge of his bunk wrestling with a knotted bootlace, heard the jarring CQD from Phillips that would precipitate a fifty-seven-mile dash on a new course—North 57 West—toward stricken *Titanic*.

Dramatically, immediately, the peaceful tenor of *Carpathia*'s onboard atmosphere was overturned. Everything changed on the instant, the hastily aroused crew galvanized as their ship started racing northward. No longer bound on a voyage of pleasure, *Carpathia* was now committed to a voyage of the most urgent purpose. Seamen's excitement inevitably infects the passenger corpus, for it is an inescapable shipboard truism that passenger and crew moods are uncontrollably contagious.

Later, Rostron was quoted by survivor Harry Barrow: "When day broke and I saw the ice I had steamed through during the night, I shuddered, and could only think that some other hand than mine was on that helm during the night."

Rostron's intensity and dedication inspired every member of his crew; no one was unaffected. Throughout *Carpathia*'s frantic repositioning they toiled everywhere. An extra stokers' watch was mustered and the amplified volume of steam their exertions produced was delivered by the chief engineer almost exclusively to the engines. But not only stokers were awake: deck gangs also set to work, breaking loose chocks securing the lifeboats. Bedroom stewards carried armloads of third class blankets down to be warmed on the boilers while their waiter colleagues converted all three dining rooms into makeshift hospitals. Electric light clusters and chair hoists were rigged at each port door and forward cargo booms were unlashed and deployed; the only steam spared from the engine room would activate their winches.

The race to *Titanic* would consume three and a half hours. Shortly after two in the morning, when the White Star vessel's radio ceased transmitting, *Carpathia* was still 34 miles away. Rostron ordered Cunard's company signals—two blue lights—sent up every quarter hour. When he neared the scene of the collision at 4 A.M., Rostron saw a green light that he hoped might be *Titanic*'s starboard riding light, indicating she was still on the surface, but it was a green flare from a lifeboat. Then, as dawn broke and the wind freshened, he began picking up survivors. It would take more than four hours to bring *Titanic*'s 703 survivors and 5 dead aboard.

Carpathia passengers, aroused by the commotion of their nighttime dash, were astonished to see through their portholes what looked like huge islands clustered in midocean. They were icebergs, an incredible assemblage stretching as far as the eye could see, a well-nigh impenetrable barrier that was already common knowledge in New York.

Carlos Hurd ran out on deck while his wife surveyed the spectacle from their cabin. She saw not only the iceberg array but, floating among them, two overturned lifeboats with figures crowded atop them. When her husband came back to tell her that *Titanic* had gone to the bottom, that same shipboard news was repeated incredulously by their stewardess, who had seen the first dazed and shivering survivors gathered in the second class dining saloon.

They had boarded from the first boat, manned largely by women. Without sufficient seamen aboard, commanding officer Boxhall could not approach *Carpathia*, so instead Rostron maneuvered his vessel closer. He could not get to windward and make a lee because an iceberg barred his way.

As the lifeboat wallowed beneath his bow, Rostron ordered Bisset and two quartermasters over the side to ensure that it would neither collide with *Carpathia* nor capsize. The three men clambered down rope ladders hung from the forward railings and, balancing nimbly along the lifeboat's thwarts, fended it aft along *Carpathia*'s frigid plating to an open port door. Once the boat had been secured alongside, its occupants either climbed or were hoisted aboard. Above them, *Carpathia* passengers lined the railings. One of the boat's occupants, Mahala Douglas, cried out hysterically, "*Titanic* has gone with everyone on board!" Brusquely, Boxhall ordered her to shut up.

Later, *Titanic* people, fortified by brandy and coffee, crowded the railings as well, searching desperately for familiar faces among ensuing boatloads. The Eustis sisters were hoisted aboard from lifeboat no. 4, entering the port door via bosun's chairs before being given hot coffee and sandwiches. When *Carpathia*'s bandmaster George Orrell learned that all *Titanic*'s musicians had perished, he was grief-stricken about Brailey and Bricoux, recent shipmates aboard the Cunarder.

After the first lifeboats had been emptied, they were hoisted up and deposited on *Carpathia*'s foredeck. Never mind the board of trade's outdated regulations—having embarked additional passengers Rostron needed additional boats.

At 8 A.M., moments after the last castaways came aboard, *Californian* appeared, nosing cautiously through the ice. An officer with signal flags on the liner's bridge wing wigwagged in all innocence to *Carpathia*: "What's the matter?" Prompted by Rostron, Bisset responded by flag: "*Titanic* hit berg and sank here with loss of 1,500 lives. Have picked up all her boats with 700 survivors. Please stay in vicinity to search for bodies." What Rostron really meant was for *Californian* to search for survivors; there was no shortage of floating dead. Dozens lay facedown on the surface, sustained by white life jackets that rendered them sometimes indistinguishable from the brash ice surrounding them.

One wonders: why was *Californian*'s signaling officer so out of the loop? Three hours earlier his chief officer had woken telegrapher Cyril Evans and, once on the air, he and Captain Lord and, one would assume, all his officers must have been made privy to the fate of "the large liner" that had mystified the previous night's bridge watch.

Rostron was burdened with command decisions. The hundreds of survivors inundating his ship—chilled, distraught, and weeping—had to be warmed, comforted, fed, and accommodated. One of *Carpathia*'s junior pursers co-opted the barbershop's supply of toothbrushes, distributing them, while they lasted, to the survivors. Another circulated with cable blanks for messages to next of kin.

The variety of those messages collected summarized, in pungent cablese, brief harrowing reports, which would be Morsed to *Olympic* for onward transmission. One to Paris read: "*Moi sauvé mais Ben perdu*" (I was saved but Ben lost). Restaurant manager Paul Maugé informed his family: "*Seul sauvé du restaurant*" (The only one saved from the restaurant), neglecting to mention the two surviving lady cashiers. To England's Pears family in Isleworth went: "Edith safe, all hope for Tom." Barkworth, a Yorkshire justice of the peace, cabled his family: "Am safe on board Carpathia, Algy." Percy, one of Isidor Straus's children, received a signal: "Every boat watched, Father, Mother not on *Carpathia*, hope still." Dozens of survivors used the rescue vessel's name as the perfect metonym for salvation—the recurring mantra "Safe Carpathia" said it all.

Cunard's house flag was lowered to half-staff and an Episcopal clergyman among *Carpathia*'s passengers led a memorial service in the dining saloon. Rostron spoke briefly, his voice breaking. Then *Carpathia* passenger Samuel Goldenburg was elected chair of a twenty-five-person Women's Relief Committee to provide funds and clothing for bereft steerage survivors.

Four deceased *Titanic* souls would be buried discreetly the following morning. A fifth was miraculously restored to life. *Titanic*'s first class barber August Weikman had spent so long immersed that, hoisted aboard in extremis, he was pronounced dead. A surgeon ordered all possessions removed from his pockets, his clothes stripped off, and the body sewn into a canvas shroud. (Thankfully, the sailor's traditional final embellishment, a stitch through the nose, was *not* administered.) Shortly thereafter Weikman miraculously came back to life, gratefully rejoining his fellow survivors.

Out on deck, seamen hauled up six more *Titanic* lifeboats, adding them to the forepeak stack; seven more had already been suspended in davits. The crated Packard was a terrible nuisance.

Attending to the survivors' immediate needs was one thing, but what to do with them? Carrying them to the Azores or Gibraltar would exhaust *Carpathia*'s linen and provisions. If Rostron made for Halifax additional ice might obstruct him. He debated handing them over to approaching *Olympic*, but subjecting *Titanic*'s fragile people to yet another midocean transfer was anathema; also, how might they react to the apparition of what seemed the liner that had just sunk beneath them?

The text of the cable that Rostron sent that morning to the Associated Press in New York advising them of *Titanic*'s loss ended "proceeding American port." Those final two words were inked out, replaced by "New York." Survivors would achieve their destination via *Carpathia* rather than *Titanic*.

Understandably, Rostron adopted a proprietary air about what he perceived as unquestionably *his* survivors; he had plucked them from the sea and was determined to protect them as much as was humanly possible, an attitude that arose, I sense, from the man's profound religious convictions.

Passage to Manhattan involved considerable discomfort. Doubled or tripled up in staterooms, camped out in public rooms, or packed into overtaxed crew cabins were the 703 rescued. It has always struck me as unreasonable how *Titanic*'s first class survivors presumed that equivalent accommodations were their due aboard the rescue ship, privileged expectation entitling them to continued first class perks on another line's vessel. If one could not occupy an actual first class cabin, one camped out in a first class public room or sat, blanket shrouded, along first class decks.

There were plenty of empty berths down in third class. If stewards could convert *Carpathia* dining saloons into makeshift hospitals, surely they could also have wrought some sort of cosmetic upgrade along those lower decks. *Titanic* cabin passengers ensconced in those humble quarters would at least have had a berth;

first class men of the period, graduates of spartan boarding schools, could easily have made do.

Yet abrogating Edwardians' entrenched class sensibilities, even in the wake of catastrophe, was never considered. Though cabin passengers used occasionally to *visit* third—"slumming" was the odious catchphrase—sleeping there was unheard of. Third class was partially occupied by those 565 old home traffic as well as *Titanic*'s crew and immigrant passengers. To become their de facto shipmates, rubbing shoulders and sharing public bathrooms, was perceived as insalubrity of the worst order.

How things had changed sixty-two years later when stranded *Queen Elizabeth 2*'s 1,648 passengers were off-loaded during another Atlantic April, in 1974. En route to the Caribbean *QE2* had lost power after a fractured oil-feed pipe contaminated her boiler water; she had been adrift for three days. Rescuer was Flagship Cruise's 20,000-ton *Sea Venture*, commanded by Captain Torbjorn Hauge, visiting Hamilton, Bermuda.

Most of his passengers were ashore; those aboard were given cash for hotel rooms because Hauge needed every berth. At 1 P.M. on 3 April, he raced *Sea Venture* 280 miles southwest, reaching Cunard's dark and disabled flagship at three o'clock the next morning. Tonnage disparity between *QE2* and *Sea Venture* was even more glaring than that separating *Titanic* from *Carpathia*. This rescue ship had only 316 cabins, now furnished with extra cots in which many of the Cunard influx would sleep. Whether first or tourist was completely academic; without friction or fuss, hundreds of grateful castaways managed.

Carpathia's crew did its best to accommodate that overwhelming invasion. *Titanic* waiters served meals in the dining saloon. Captain Rostron gave up his quarters to the widows of three millionaires. Second officer Lightoller did not need a cabin. A devout Christian Scientist, he claimed that he stayed awake for the entire four-day passage to New York. And this from a man who had nearly been dragged below with *Titanic*, then spent hours in the water, laboring to keep two dozen men alive on an overturned collapsible.

Throughout the little Cunarder, formerly neglected spaces were pressed into service. Colin Cooper, the *Tribune* artist, surrendered his cabin to three women survivors, among them widowed Renée Harris. The Eustis sisters were accommodated in a four-berth inside normally used as a dressing room; one of the pair sharing that poky little space was fellow lifeboat passenger Mrs. Cummings, the other widowed Mrs. Astor's maid.

Martha Eustis Stephenson described conditions aboard overcrowded *Carpathia*: "We lived on deck as there was no place to sit inside the ship. Bouillon on deck and sometimes two or three sittings in the dining saloon. We had no appetite; still the menu was the same as on all steamers." That would change; food shortages surfaced toward New York and tea biscuits ran out completely.

Harold Cottam spent hours in *Carpathia*'s radio room, later assuring Senator William Alden Smith at the Senate hearings that he was "the only operator on board and was on duty nearly all the time." Not strictly true. He was assisted by *Titanic*'s severely injured surviving telegrapher. The two Harolds—Bride and Cottam—tried sending the names of all survivors to *Olympic*, whose more powerful wireless room could relay transmissions to either shore as she waited, stationary in the North Atlantic, before being ordered to resume course for Southampton.

No other vessel picked up anyone. Ironically, crewmen aboard Sable Island's chartered cable ship *Minia*, thought at one point to have embarked some who had survived, would later help retrieve many who had patently not, hauling dozens of bodies from the waters off Cape Race into their dories.

In London, inaccuracy and grief predominated. The London *Times* of 16 April insisted stubbornly that all *Titanic*'s passengers had been rescued and were safely aboard *Carpathia* and *Parisian*. Two days later, the Lord Mayor's Fund for *Titanic*'s dead was inaugurated with £950 in donations from Their Majesties. The royal family also attended a packed memorial service in St. Paul's Cathedral with some five thousand worshippers. When the choir sang "For Those in Peril on the Sea," Harland and Wolff's Alexander Carlisle was so overcome he collapsed.

Ever since the initial reports, New Yorkers had been plagued by three days' worth of hopeful speculation, coupled with increasingly preposterous reassurance. Although Reuters amended its earlier bulletin that no lives had been lost, General Philip Franklin, the only American among IMM's trio of vice presidents, not only had no information, he also seemed incapable of comprehending the scope of the calamity. "Passengers," he insisted initially, "were in no great danger." One of Franklin's subsequent announcements quoted him as suggesting that the vessel's passengers "had been taken off by *Carpathia*, *Virginian*, *Parisian* and *Olympic*, which rushed to the aid of her sister." He also cabled Ismay aboard *Carpathia*: "Concise Marconigram account of actual accident greatly needed for enlightenment. Public and ourselves. This is most important."

There was no response. In fact, Ismay had composed a Marconigram on the fifteenth, outlining the tragedy and pulling no punches: "Deeply regret advise you *Titanic* sank this morning fifteenth after collision iceberg serious loss life further particulars later Bruce Ismay."

Inexplicably, that message would not be dispatched for two more days; moreover, those "further particulars" never appeared. White Star's devastated managing director seldom emerged from sedation in surgeon McGee's cabin.

Grasping at straws, Franklin temporized unconvincingly to relatives besieging White Star's office at Bowling Green. After he finally admitted the calamitous loss of life, those frantic family members abandoned their White Star vigil, turning their attention instead to Cunard's booking office a few doors north. But precious little satisfaction was available there. Cunard's North American manager Charles Sumner blamed Rostron for remaining stubbornly incommunicado aboard approaching *Carpathia*. By the morning of 17 April, although every New York paper acknowledged her as the only vessel carrying survivors, repeated wireless inquiries had aroused no response. Some of the silence during daylight hours may have been legitimate because of her limited range. Later, Bride would confess to *New York Times* reporter James Speers that he saw no reason to answer press inquiries when he and Cottam were preoccupied dispatching survivor traffic.

Even Marconi put his oar in, sending explicit reproofs to his operators aboard *Carpathia*. His first penciled signal read imperiously: "Wire news dispatches immediately. If this is impossible, ask captain why there is no news available. Guglielmo Marconi"

Had he been able, one *Carpathia* passenger would have been delighted to respond. Reporter Carlos Hurd was determined to interview survivors so that he could deliver a worldwide scoop the moment *Carpathia* reached New York. He tried enlisting the help of Cooper, his *Tribune* colleague, but was rejected. "I'm not interested. I'm on my vacation," the man responded. So Hurd dragooned his wife, Katherine, into gathering and recording surviving women's accounts. Whereas Carlos was restricted from entering their quarters, Katherine was free to do so while he, in turn, interviewed the men. The couple began amassing material for a long, comprehensive story.

Remembrance of the *St. Louis Post-Dispatch* reporter's presence on board had not escaped the *New York World*'s omniscient Chapin. He cabled Hurd and told him that he would be meeting *Carpathia* aboard New York tug *Dalzelline*, a signal Hurd never received, doubtless suppressed on Rostron's orders.

Once his spiral notebooks were filled, Hurd scribbled on additional sheets of paper. Determined as the reporter was to complete his story, Rostron was equally determined to make it impossible. Unable to prohibit Hurd's access to survivors, he tried depriving him of the tools of his trade. Every sheet of ship's letter paper was removed from the Hurds' cabin and also from racks throughout the vessel, released only to bona fide letter writers. Hurd managed to beg some sheets from sympathetic fellow passengers.

His cabin was repeatedly searched. If the Hurds were present when the master-at-arms knocked, Katherine's strategy was to either sit stubbornly on her husband's notes in the cabin's only chair or leave with the pages pinned to her undergarments. At night, she slept with them concealed in her nightgown.

Carlos Hurd took his completed five-thousand-word dispatch and wrapped it in oilcloth before securing the bundle with string. (History does not relate how or where Hurd found either the oilcloth or the string.) Sympathetic *Titanic* survivor Spencer Silverthorne fashioned what he described as a "buoy," made from an empty cigar box. For additional buoyancy, Hurd filled the box with champagne corks cadged from barmen before attaching it with additional string to his precious bundle of pages. It was ready for delivery on the evening of 18 April when inbound *Carpathia* steamed past New York's Ambrose Channel lightship and slowed for rendezvous with the pilot boat.

Afraid that reporters concealed aboard the pilot boat might bribe their way aboard, Rostron devised an ingenious counterstrategy. Long before the Jacob's ladder was dropped from *Carpathia*'s port door—the same one through which hundreds of survivors had clambered only days earlier—he ordered the bosun to bolt two eye rings with attached lengths of marlin to each end of its bottom rung. The moment the pilot started his ascent, crewmen stationed above reeled in the marlin, effectively rolling up the ladder behind him.

So far so good. *Carpathia* proceeded up The Narrows beneath torrential rain. Lightning flashes penetrated the murk as she anchored off Staten Island's quarantine. Despite a preliminary announcement that, since the inbound Cunarder had called at no ports since her departure, inbound formalities would be waived, that earlier assurance had been rescinded. In the event, New York port regulations were not relaxed. The moment he anchored, Rostron shored up his defenses yet again, posting a seaman with a fire hose at the head of the companionway, ready to repel any reporter trying to sneak aboard. The only one who managed to embark was hustled to the bridge and put on his honor to speak to no one.

Then Rostron ordered *Carpathia*'s anchor raised and steamed slowly up harbor past the Battery, where thousands of soaked New Yorkers craned for a glimpse of the inbound vessel. It was not easy, for she was surrounded by swarms of chartered tugs, tenders, and launches jostling to accompany her upstream. Rather than wait at Pier 54, dozens of reporters were streaming down harbor, bent on wresting firsthand survivor interviews however they could.

Among that predatory fleet was *Dalzelline*, New York's largest and fastest tug, chartered by the *World* with Chapin pacing back and forth on her forepeak. She maneuvered alongside *Carpathia* so that Chapin could scan the faces lining Promenade Deck's portside railing, but finding Hurd was not easy.

By the same token, both Hurds had difficulty picking out Chapin. Having never received his Marconigram, Carlos had no idea on which vessel to look. The waters flanking *Carpathia* were chockablock with small craft, their vociferous occupants determined to either embark or persuade survivors to jump overboard. Shouting and cursing, soaked by rain, they maneuvered through a free-for-all of rivalry, confusion, and reckless boat handling.

Carpathia's Promenade Deck was packed with passengers and crew, the former on the Hurds' side, the latter aggressively not.

With the precious buoyed dispatch concealed beneath his overcoat, Carlos was hard-pressed to find a vantage point where he could be recognized by Chapin.

Finally, *Dalzelline*'s skipper shouldered his vessel through the fray and came directly alongside, colliding with the Cunarder and further antagonizing her crew. Then Chapin saw Hurd and bawled for him to throw down his dispatch. Spotting the editor in turn, Carlos extracted his precious bundle, leaned out, and hurled it toward the tug's bow. But it fouled on a line hanging from *Carpathia*'s upper deck, dangling in midair tantalizingly out of reach. Urged by an officer, a seaman reached out to grasp it but, in tweaking the line, he inadvertently let the bundle drop into Chapin's hands. Passengers cheered.

Once Chapin held his trophy aloft so his skipper could see it, *Dalzelline*'s helm was ported abruptly. She broke clear and, turning in a tight circle, boiled toward the Battery. Once there, Chapin ordered a subordinate, Ross Whytock, to commandeer a taxi and carry the story to the office. But every Manhattan cab, it seemed, was besieging Pier 54, so Whytock ran through the rain to waiting printmen at the plant. Hurd's scoop was on the street, adorning the front page of that evening's *New York World* before *Carpathia* tied up.

The scene along drenched Twelfth Avenue was chaotic. Taxis and cars were stalled in long lines, horns hooting and drivers swearing as they tried negotiating passage through crowds overflowing the sidewalks. Police contingents from several precincts, doing their best to keep order, estimated that thirty thousand New Yorkers had swamped Pier 54's approaches. The worst offenders were reporters and journalists; just as their colleagues had flocked downstream to accompany *Carpathia*, so they laid siege to Twelfth Avenue's pier frontage.

The focus of the frantic crowds, gallant little *Carpathia*, tied up in the pier's northern slip at 9:35 P.M., the opposite side from which she had sailed exactly a week earlier. With the possible exception of returning troopships, no other Manhattan landfall would foment such a frenetic response. With her amplified passenger load, *Carpathia* assumed an inescapable role, no longer the ship of widows but the ship of truth, those additional souls aboard the only living residue of *Titanic*'s passenger load. Every New York flag, both aboard ships or upon buildings ashore, flew at half-staff.

Survivors would disembark carrying nothing, like Staten Island commuters; all they owned, they wore. When the gangway was rigged, they had to confront the maelstrom inside the pier shed, packed with desperately anxious relatives. Their descent, one by one, into that angst-ridden, brightly illuminated arena would arouse contrasting reactions, unpredictable lady-or-the-tiger finales. It was that brutally simple.

The appearance of living survivors precipitated scenes of joyful, incredulous relief and reunion. Tears were commonplace, juxtaposed with wails of grief, swooning women, and unbridled hysteria. Once the last of the passengers—men, women, and children—had been welcomed, heartbreaking absence dictated the rest. Hundreds had to accept the awful realization that their loved ones had drowned; if they had not materialized on *Carpathia*'s gangway, they never would.

The most celebrated visitor to Pier 54 that night was Guglielmo Marconi. In terms of public relations, he found himself in an awkward position. The price of his company's stock had quadrupled since the news broke and he did not want to be perceived as profiting from disaster. Yet at the same time, he was furious and mystified by inbound *Carpathia*'s silence.

He left Holland House, traveling south on the elevated train as far as Forty-second Street before transferring to a taxi provided by the *New York Times*. Near Fourteenth Street's monumental traffic jam, a police sergeant recognized the vehicle's famous occupant and warned him that no cabs would be admitted to the pier. But the sergeant's superior, a lieutenant, promised to escort Marconi inside on foot.

When not in use, New York piers are inevitably moribund. Only for ship arrivals or departures do they come to echoing life—ship's winches working baggage and cargo, shouting stevedores, petulant passengers and their querulous visitors, and choruses of farewell or greeting played out against the resonating thunder of iron-wheeled barrows laden with crates and trunks.

That night of nights, though, conventional clamor had been reduced to uneasy dirge. Floods of survivors and their families, outnumbered by the disappointed, made their doleful way toward Twelfth Avenue, many of them weeping and distraught. The spectacle of so much human suffering was overwhelming. Such was the outpouring of grief that Marconi, struggling against that human tide, was himself reduced to tears.

Among the first survivors they encountered emerging from one of the freight elevators was Astor's widow Madeleine, escorted by her stepson Vincent Astor and accompanied by two doctors and a nurse. She went uptown by limousine to call on her ailing father. Four years later she would marry William K. Dick in Bar Harbor.

Marconi and the lieutenant finally reached Pier 54's upper level and embarked aboard *Carpathia*. Approaching the radio shack, Marconi immediately picked out the familiar crackle of spark gaps. Inside, Harold Bride was perched on the edge of Cottam's empty bunk, his bandaged feet propped on a chair. Doggedly, he was still transmitting, trying to clear the backlog of survivors' messages.

The young telegrapher turned and saw the great Guglielmo Marconi in the flesh for the first time, standing on the threshold. Bride, whom Marconi thought looked like a ghost, was exhausted and deeply distressed. "You know, Mr. Marconi," were his first halting words, "Phillips is dead."

His annoyance defused, Marconi entered, shook hands solemnly, and, after a moment's hesitation, sat companionably next to Bride on the bunk. He inquired gently about his injured feet and then listened to his young employee's rambling but coherent report. It all spilled out, from the first CQD, *Titanic*'s foundering, his ordeal on the overturned collapsible, the impact of Phillips's death—Bride's guilt in that regard was palpable—and the enervating westbound sea days that had followed.

Marconi posed some technical questions about the reliability of *Carpathia*'s wireless and then, probing further, asked whether, en route to New York, he had talked with reporters.

Hotly, Bride denied responding to any journalists: "They sounded so curt and demanding in tone that I shut them off and went ahead sending out personal messages." Then, his voice quavering, he returned yet again to the painful subject of drowned Phillips.

"Did he freeze to death?" inquired Marconi.

"I think he did, sir," responded Bride. "If only I could have slipped more clothing on Phillips. I slipped on an overcoat and life jacket but I ought to have put on still more."

The two men, the Nobel-winning laureate and his very junior telegrapher, might have talked through the night but for the arrival of ambulance men from Saint Vincent's Hospital with a wheelchair to take Bride ashore; he would be *Carpathia*'s last disembarking survivor. Marconi did not even bother confronting Rostron; the specter of poor Bride told him all he needed to know.

Cunard was determined that *Carpathia* would resume her aborted cruise at 4:00 P.M. the following afternoon, less than twenty-four hours after tying up. It would precipitate a brutal turnaround schedule for the crew, already stressed by their extra inbound passengers, followed now by a second inundation of reporters, visitors, and relatives storming the pier.

Once surviving passengers had gone ashore, 210 *Titanic* officers and crew were mustered and disembarked through pressing throngs, marching raggedly to the Chelsea piers to embark aboard Red Star's *Lapland* for passage home. As they proceeded up Twelfth Avenue, reporters badgered them. Though cautioned not to speak to any, trimmer James Frank Avery could not resist telling one aggressive journalist that he had been in the sea for more than an hour. "How was it?" the reporter demanded. "Cold!" retorted Avery before hastening to rejoin his mates.

The following morning the crew were issued replacement uniforms. Wearing them, many attended a memorial service at the American Seamen's Friends Society at 100 West Street. Then they returned to *Lapland*. Crowding the ship's lobby was a group of *Titanic* stewardesses in floods of tears. Their male colleagues gathered on the vessel's forepeak, exhausted and grim. Sailing with them were passengers originally booked on the eastbound leg of *Titanic*'s maiden voyage, who were using the Red Star vessel as a convenient substitute.

Though nearly all her cruise passengers remained aboard *Carpathia* that night, there was little sleep for them and less for the hard-pressed crew. Too early, the familiar refrain echoed throughout crew country: "Rise and shine for the Cunard Line!" The vessel's interiors were chaotic: discarded bedding, mattresses, blankets, and pillows littered every public room. Tackling the mess, some crewmen found *Titanic* life jackets and cut them open for keepsakes. One souvenir cork block ended up, by request, in Augusta Ogden's cabin.

Urgently needed were laundry, provisions, and coal. Rather than await a fresh set of *Carpathia* linen from Cunard's contracted Manhattan launderer, marine superintendent Roberts arranged with nearby *Saxonia*'s chief steward that her allotment of fresh sheets, towels, tablecloths, and napkins be transferred to *Carpathia*.

Coal was nearly exhausted. Though *Carpathia* had sailed with full bunkers on the eleventh, she had steamed eastbound for three and a half days and completed that coal-rich northern detour before persevering another three and a half days back to New York. Towed up from Perth Amboy, coal barges arrived in the slip early next morning. Once the vessel had been boomed away from the pier, tons of Pennsylvania anthracite rattled into her depleted bunkers, awaking every passenger on board.

Normally, coaling a vessel remains an exclusive operation; neither provisions nor laundry can be loaded at the same time because of coal dust. But nothing about *Carpathia*'s inhuman deadline approximated normalcy. Dust notwithstanding, laundry and provisions were hastened indiscriminately aboard at the same time. More work for the hard-pressed crew, washing and wiping down gritty dust fouling every interior ledge and shelf.

All day on the nineteenth, hordes of curious New Yorkers descended on the vessel. They knew no passengers, they just wanted to set foot aboard *Carpathia* and poke their noses into the empty wireless shack. Cottam was sleeping the sleep of the dead somewhere in third class and Bride was ashore in the hospital.

Only one couple from *Carpathia*'s original occupants decided not to stay on board for the cruise. So she sailed with an almost identical passenger list, all of them as anxious as was Cunard for resumption of their interrupted eastbound voyage. At 4 P.M., once bellboys' gongs had cleared cabins, alleyways, and public rooms, as many *Carpathia* visitors who could crowded onto Pier 54's apron to wave her off.

Her hawsers slipped, the little Cunarder proceeded sternfirst into the Hudson and, with a tug beneath her port bow, was turned downstream. An exhausted Rostron, standing on the port bridge wing, doffed his cap in acknowledgment of sustained applause and cheers from shore. Heading seaward once more with only her legitimate passenger load, *Carpathia* resumed workaday service, her exemplary mission concluded.

Throughout passenger country, by mutual consent, it was agreed that *Titanic* as a conversational subject was not only exhausted but should be taboo. But it was doubtful that any such embargo would be observed aboard *Carpathia* for years. The vessel had been touched by history, key participant in the most egregious maritime disaster of all time. There would be medals, awards, and remembrances aplenty in the days to come. "Molly" Brown struck a special *Carpathia* medal, in gold for the master, silver for his officers, and bronze for every crew member. Throughout the Mediterranean, crowds in every port would fete those same men. By a unanimous act of Congress, Rostron would be presented with a gold medal, pinned to his chest by a grateful President Taft.

Carpathia's end came on 17 July 1918 when, like so many unsung wartime carriers, in a sixteen-ship convoy, she was struck by two torpedoes 120 miles west of Fastnet. After her 250 passengers had entered the lifeboats, their stricken vessel remained afloat until a third torpedo sent her to the bottom. Because of her pivotal role in the events of 15 April 1912, "unsung" can scarcely characterize at least one remarkable episode of *Carpathia*'s time line.

A few months earlier, in March 1918, as part of a draft of doughboys embarking aboard troopship *Mauretania* in New York, Second Lieutenant Arnold Robert was headed for Brest and the trenches. An accomplished linguist, he served as regimental interpreter and, as such, was privy to all staff meetings en route. Once the dazzle-painted Cunarder had swept into the darkened seaway beyond the Ambrose lightship, her master convened every American officer in the ship's library. His opening remarks were deadly earnest yet, once the man's identity had been made clear, perhaps to be expected.

"Gentlemen," he began, "I am not anticipating trouble, but in the event of an emergency, I shall expect every one of you to do his utmost."

He was Captain Arthur Rostron, former master of *Carpathia*.

CHAPTER 8

CREW MEMORIA

Poignant in a different way was the fate of the personnel of the A la Carte restaurant. Largely Italian and French, they seem to have had no chance at all—only three were saved.

Walter Lord, *A Night to Remember*

That's just the bestest band that am, Honey Lamb . . .

Irving Berlin, "Alexander's Ragtime Band," 1911

Titanic's loss precipitated an orgy of remembrance. In addition to a deluge of documentary books, there were memorials, plaques, plinths, church windows, and elaborate tombs for the recovered deceased. There were other outpourings as well—paintings, needlepoints, musical compositions, and reams of poetry. Thousands, from amateur scribblers to Thomas Hardy and Joseph Conrad, felt moved to write. Others sculpted, modeled, stitched, composed, or fabricated something, anything to convey the extent of their grief.

Perhaps the sinking of White Star's vessel in mid–maiden voyage ranks as one of the two most devastating events of 1912. The other unquestionably would have been the death of Captain Robert Scott's five-man party en route home from the South Pole, to which they had been preceded by Norwegian spoiler Roald Amundsen. The impact of these twin losses equaled that of 9/11 in our time, although the tragic distinction separating 1912 from 2001 was that human villainy rather than nature toppled Manhattan's World Trade Center towers.

That they were destroyed in an accessible municipal locus meant that a much-debated memorial will be erected at ground zero. No such on-site commemoration was possible for the more than 1,500 who perished at 41° 46′ North, 50° 14′ West a century ago. The only acknowledgments were transitory as passing steamships of many nationalities paused over the wreck and cast memorial wreaths into the sea. Among those now vanished maritime mourners, only the International Ice Patrol, established after and because of *Titanic*'s foundering, and America's Titanic Historical Society still perpetuate that once common ritual, though from aircraft rather than ship. Throughout the 1920s, on the anniversary of her husband's death, Commodore Edward Smith's widow, Eleanor, would present a red rose to every *Olympic* bridge officer.

In this chapter, we shall dwell on victims among the crew. Whereas passenger losses triggered outpourings of grief around the globe, those who would have become the vessel's permanent inhabitants represented an evocative nautical focus in Britain and, to a lesser extent, on the continent. RMS *Titanic* was not only White Star's newest liner, but she also would have served as unique domicile, crew workplace and home combined. Of course, they had other homes as well, in Liverpool and Southampton for triweekly reunions with wives and children, but most of their days would have been spent together at sea, thundering to New York and back.

As aboard every ocean liner, *Titanic* passengers were accommodated in several classes. One would have thought that crew members who perished, whether on bridge or passenger decks or in stokehold, would have been grouped posthumously within classless unanimity, granted an equality denied them in life. Regrettably, they were not. Examination of various memorials derails that democratic ideal, revealing that shipboard rankings were consistently and unblinkingly maintained.

Just over two years after the tragedy, on 22 April 1914, *Titanic*'s most famous memorial was unveiled in Southampton, its committee chaired by retired Royal Naval Reserve captain F .J. Blake. Called the Engineers Memorial, its £2,000 cost had been underwritten by donations from merchant marine engineers around the world, contributions quite naturally spurred by the deaths of all *Titanic*'s engineering officers. Not for nothing "the sailor king," His Majesty George V was so distressed by the toll he decreed that, thenceforth, Britain's Merchant and Royal Naval engineers would wear a field of purple between the gold stripes on their sleeves, commemorating their drowned White Star colleagues. So strongly did the monarch's concern resonate internationally that all the world's royal and merchant navies followed suit; so too would airline engineers to come.

Many have felt that Commodore Smith's two most egregious errors that night were, first, maintaining speed despite multiple radioed ice warnings and, second, dismissing his two Marconi operators but neglecting to do the same for his engineers. Thirty-two men (or thirty-five, depending on which memorial's listing you read) were drowned. Though many dozen stokers, trimmers, and greasers found their way into lifeboats, not one of their officers did. Additional engineering loss was Harland and Wolff's ten-man inspection team. Formally headed by Archibald Frost, its putative leader was unquestionably *Titanic*'s naval architect, Thomas Andrews.

Planning, erecting, and completing a memorial is challenging. After municipal authorities have provided a site, a sometimes contentious committee raises funds, hires architect and sculptor, and decides which names to memorialize. Once it has been unveiled and dedicated, the creative team moves on to other commissions, the committee disbands, and its members gradually die off. But the edifice they have jointly wrought remains in place essentially forever. Choices hammered out in preparatory fervor have been cast or chiseled, literally, in bronze, granite, or marble. As we well know, anent the extraordinarily emotional power of Maya Lin's Vietnam Veterans Memorial in Washington, it is sometimes less the monument or sculpture than the inscribed names that remain its most compelling components.

The Engineers Memorial was built in a gentle crescent at one corner of Andrews Park, readily visible from the sidewalk as well as by occupants of vehicular traffic; a major crossroad lies only yards away. Designed by architect Joseph Whitehead, it was enriched by statuary of the London-based Swiss sculptor Ferdinand Victor Blundstone. The Aberdeeen granite colonnade is 32½ feet (10 meters) wide and 19 feet (5.7 meters) tall, with a depth of 9 feet (2.7 meters).

Rising above Whiteside's central arching entablature is Blundstone's largest heraldic figure, Glory. She stands sorrowfully atop a vessel's protruding prow, her anatomy revealed by the fluidity of a diaphanous, clinging garment. Linking the celestial with the hyperrealistic, each of Glory's outstretched hands holds a laurel wreath, which, with bowed head, she proffers to two men toiling within rectangular sculpted panels below, bas-relief windows into desperation. Striving for maritime exactitude, the sculptor has recreated portions of *Titanic*'s engine rooms, complete with valves, control wheels, cogs, radial arms, cabling, bolt heads, rivets, piping, and tanks. *Olympic*-class vessels were powered by combined technologies: two four-cylinder, triple-expansion reciprocating engines driving outboard propellers while a steam turbine turned a third propeller between them.

Blundstone's two figures are posed on what engineers call the starting platform, the left-hand one for a turbine, the right for one of the reciprocating engines. Revealed in its entirety, the figure on the left sports a luxuriant mustache. He is clad in peaked cap and uniform tunic, his visible right sleeve unmistakably adorned with four stripes. The sculptor has elevated the angle of his subject's head so that a resolute profile faces right. The pose seems somehow forced, features and distinctive mustache displayed to advantage yet, at the same time, rendering the man curiously detached from the task that should be preoccupying him.

If identifiable engineers were to inhabit his memorial, small wonder that Blundstone selected the two most senior. Since only one four-stripe engineer serves aboard any vessel, the sculptor has obviously portrayed *Titanic*'s chief engineer Joseph Bell, that Elgar-like mustache the clincher. Only fifty-one, Bell grew up in the Cumberland village of Farlam where he left a widow and four children. The oldest, at sixteen and a half already a Harland and Wolff engineering apprentice, had sailed with his father aboard *Titanic* from Belfast as far as Southampton.

We see Bell grasping a turbine's radial control arm identified by one of several plaques. The largest announces TURBINE STEAM, and the arm he is manipulating rests halfway between the legends AHEAD and STOP; ASTERN is concealed by his head. Bell's ungloved grip is determined, right hand cupped upward beneath the handle, while the fingers of his left cover and reinforce the right.

It is difficult to tell whether he is pulling or pushing the lever through its arc. One assumes he must be pulling, as though retarding admission of steam into the turbine casing. If that were the sculptor's intent, he has provided us with a precise time line: 11:41 P.M. on the night of 14 April 1912, moments after officer of the watch William Murdoch has rung FULL ASTERN on the bridge telegraph, an abrupt and unusual command in midocean near midnight.

Yet however dramatically Blundstone has depicted the chief, his mise-en-scène is wishful thinking: *Titanic*'s turbines could *not* be reversed. Exclusively turbine-driven ships such as *Lusitania* and *Mauretania* had substantial astern power because they boasted a second set of opposing turbines; the primary ones steamed forward and the secondaries were used exclusively for retrogression astern. That is the only way rotation of a turbine shaft can be changed, by switching gears and deploying preexisting turbines specifically installed for the task.

In addition to lacking astern capability, *Titanic*'s turbine-driven central propeller was a weak sister. It never started revolving until sufficient steam had implemented forward motion for her flanking reciprocating engines. If the vessel had to be maneuvered astern in port, her turbine-driven propeller merely freewheeled idly, useless until resumption of forward momentum was rung down from the bridge. Clearly, Blundstone never consulted a knowledgeable marine engineer before transforming malleable clay into unforgiving bronze; his Chief Bell is portrayed grappling with a mechanical impossibility.

That both men wear dress uniforms on starting platforms is odd; duty engineers never would. By the same token, neither had stood an engine room watch for years. They serve instead as allegorical commanders, posthumously reenacting maneuvers their subordinates had performed that night.

Steam reciprocating engines are reversible and, in the right-hand panel, we see another officer from behind, his head craned upward. He is clean-shaven and a tantalizingly indeterminate number of stripes—perhaps three and a half?—appear on both sleeves. This must be the senior second engineer William Farquharson, second in command to the chief. Farquharson was a Liverpudlian, son of a shipping executive with T. G. Royden & Co., survived by a widow and three children.

He has been portrayed realistically and accurately, in the midst of implementing a similarly demanding procedure. He peers upward while furiously cranking the handle of a small overhead valve wheel with his upraised right hand. His left rests momentarily on a large wheel of the kind commonly used to admit or prohibit steam from entering a reciprocating engine's pistons.

That large wheel is the only sculptural anomaly despoiling Blundstone's right-hand panel. Circumference and spokes alike seem more akin to the flat, steel-rimmed wheel of a farm implement than the rounded, hand-friendly valve wheels commonplace in engine rooms. Positioning his wheel vertically rather than in protruding horizontal mode, as it would have been, the sculptor has accommodated it to his depth limitations; reproducing it in that alien rural configuration was a second preventable error.

The memorial has one odd provision, perhaps pressed on architect Whitehead by Captain Blake's committee. To either side, directly beneath those engine room views, granite benches have been carved into the structure. Seated on them, viewers could contemplate the monument only with difficulty; instead, they became part of it.

Inscriptions abound. Directly beneath the angel is a familiar verse from St. John's Gospel.

GREATER LOVE HATH NO MAN THAN
THIS: THAT A MAN LAY DOWN HIS
LIFE FOR HIS FRIENDS

Below that, the granite is inscribed:

TO THE MEMORY OF THE ENGINEER OFFICERS
OF THE R.M.S. "TITANIC" WHO SHOWED
THEIR HIGH CONCEPTION OF DUTY AND THEIR
HEROISM BY REMAINING AT THEIR POSTS
15 APRIL 1912

This particular *dédicase* reads badly, patently the work of divided committee members who lumbered disparate points of view into one awkward sentence, committing unwieldy prose to the ages.

The bottom entry acknowledges the contributors.

ERECTED BY THEIR FELLOW ENGINEERS AND FRIENDS
THROUGHOUT THE WORLD

To the left, in the granite directly below Chief Bell, are incised the first twenty names of *Titanic*'s engineering staff. Headed by Bell and Farquharson, their order adheres scrupulously to rank, from chief through second, third, fourth, fifth, and sixth engineers, concluding with six electricians, two boilermakers, and a plumber.

Although the second allotment of fifteen officers continues on a right-hand panel, there is no acknowledgment of the scores of stokers, trimmers, and greasers who also lost their lives; officers only are memorialized. The same discrimination colors a too-brief, chiseled addenda, as much an afterthought as *Titanic*'s third propeller.

ALSO:
THOMAS ANDREWS   ARCHIBALD FROST
ROBERT KNIGHT

Here, again, seniority counted. Only the three top men of Harland and Wolff's ten-man team made the cut. The seven that did not are remembered here: outside foreman engineer Anthony Frost, draftsman Roderick Chisholm (the lifeboat designer), the electrical department's assistant manager William Parr, and four apprentices—electrician Ennis Watson, joiner William Campbell, fitter Alfred Cunningham, and plumber Francis Parkes.

This neglect of humbler participants is at odds, for example, with a bronze memorial tablet affixed to the pedestal supporting London's Cleopatra's Needle, the granite obelisk housed in an iron tube called *Cleopatra* and towed by a seagoing tug from Alexandria to Gravesend. The names of six tug crewmen who drowned attempting to rescue their *Cleopatra* shipmates during a storm are spelled out in full.

All the Harland and Wolff group could easily have been included, for blank granite aplenty remains along the facade; moreover, symmetry, that inescapable Edwardian fixation, could easily have been retained. Transferring seven officers' names from the right-hand list to the left would have left more than adequate room for the balance of the shipyard roster. But the memorial's committeemen were apparently determined to winnow those civilian names as well, commemorating only those of officer status rather than NCO or other ranks.

The Engineers Memorial was unveiled by Sir Archibald Denny, president of the Marine Engineers Institute, on 22 April 1914. In attendance was a crowd of ten thousand, including dozens of crew widows and their children. Before Sir Archibald unveiled the monument, it was temporarily concealed beneath a huge, draped Union Jack.

Name counts differ from memorial to memorial. The Glasgow *Titanic* Engineers Memorial, inscribed on a marble plaque and surmounted by twin female nudes, still hangs in the lobby of 39 Elmbank Crescent, present-day headquarters of Scottish Opera. The building began life in 1907 as the Institute of Engineers and Shipbuilders of Scotland, a beaux arts structure designed by John Bennie Wilson. Two Glaswegians among the names are those of William Mackie and William Kelly, the latter an assistant electrical engineer who sailed aboard *Titanic* to finish up incomplete fitting out from Belfast. In toto, Glasgow's roll of honor contains thirty-two names, three fewer than the thirty-five memorialized in Southampton. Neither junior third engineer Edward Dodd, senior fourth engineer Leonard Hodgkinson, nor William Duffy, an engineer department clerk, can be found incised on Glasgow's marble.

Yet another *Titanic* engineers' memorial plaque hangs above a staircase turn at London's Institute of Marine Engineers headquarters at 80 Coleman Street. It is topped by the figure of Triton, driving an unlikely team of four polar bears. Below, beneath a representation of sinking *Titanic*, thirty-eight names are listed, headed by Joseph Bell and continuing alphabetically. Sculpted figures to either side seem replications of Blundstone's starting platform themes from the Southampton memorial, though their roles have been reversed: on the right, Bell grasps an engine room telegraph while an officer on the left—probably Farquharson again—manipulates that nonexistent radial arm for the turbines.

The loss of all the officers of a single *Titanic* department created the impetus for Southampton's memorial. Of *Titanic*'s 898 crew members, 212 survived. For the balance of those men and women not memorialized on the Engineers Memorial, a Firemen's and Crew Memorial drinking fountain was erected a year later, an elaborate Portland stone structure located at the south end of Southampton Common. By 1972 it had been so badly vandalized that it was removed and reerected within a gated enclosure in the ruins of bombed-out Holy Rood Church in the city.

In Belfast, an elaborate *Titanic* memorial drinking fountain was erected at the intersection of Donegall Square North and Chichester Street. Deemed a traffic hazard by the mid-1980s, it was removed to City Hall's greensward, becoming one of a triumvirate, joining sculpted memorials to Sir Edward Harland and Viscount William Pirrie.

No longer a drinking fountain, the *Titanic* memorial is crowned high overhead by four marble figures. Once again, Glory reigns supreme, wearing and holding laurel wreaths that she proffers to the central figure of a trio afloat in the waves at her feet, a dead or unconscious seaman supported by two nude female swimmers. The granite plinth bears the legend:

TITANIC MEMORIAL

Erected to the imperishable memory
of the heroic Belfast men whose
names are here inscribed and who
lost their lives on the 15th April 1912
by the foundering of the Belfast built
R.M.S. *Titanic* through collision with
an iceberg on her maiden voyage
from Southampton to New York

On the plinth's left-hand side are inscribed eleven names.

Thomas Andrews, Jr.
William Henry Marsh Parr
Roderick Chisholm
Anthony Wood Frost
Robert Knight
William Campbell
Ennis Hastings Watson
Francis Parkes
Alfred Fleming Cunningham
Herbert Gifford Harvey
Albert George Ervine

The first nine names list Harland and Wolff's inspection team but the name of its putative leader, Archibald Frost—obviously not a Belfast man—has been omitted. The last two names, Messrs. Harvey and Ervine, were *Titanic* engineers.

On the opposite, right side eleven more Belfast names appear.

Dr. John Edward Simpson
William McReynolds
Henry Philip Creese

Thomas Millar
Hugh Fitzpatrick
Joseph Beattie
Matthew Leonard
Archibald Scott
Hugh Calderwood
Richard Turley
William McQuillan

The first, Simpson, was *Titanic*'s assistant surgeon, and the next four, McReynolds through Fitzpatrick, are engineering officers. The remaining six, all but steward Matthew Leonard, were juniors in the engineering department, three firemen, a greaser, and a trimmer.

Other departmental losses were just as grievous as the engineers and, one might have thought, equally worthy of commemoration. For instance, of the sixty-nine crewmen and -women employed in *Titanic*'s A la Carte restaurant, only three survived, one man and two women: maître d'hôtel Paul Maugé and lady cashiers Martin and Bowker. The remaining sixty-six—nearly twice the number of engineering officers—were drowned.

Those restaurant dead were almost exclusively waiters and sous chefs, most of them foreigners to boot. White Star's Cherbourg agents, Messieurs Le Pont and Le Niece, had worried about that largely French or Italian restaurant staff, who they opined may have resigned themselves to the bleak expectation that "only members of the crew able to work the boats would embark with the rescued passengers."

One, and one only, departmental group survived in toto, the six QMs (quartermasters) who either served as helmsmen on the bridge or were posted on the after docking bridge; in an emergency, each was assigned to a lifeboat. Not so the ship's corps of three bellboys, all teenagers but not strictly qualifying as children. Masters A. Barratt, Clifford Harris, and W. A. Watson did not survive, nor did Charles Turvey, A la Carte's sole page boy.

Titanic's most poignantly remembered departmental dead were her eight bandsmen, including: Wallace Hartley, leader and violinist; pianist Theodore Brailey; violist Georges Krins; cellist Roger Bricoux; and bassist John Clarke. These five formed a piano quintet assigned to the Reception Room on the threshold of the first class restaurant. The remaining three made up the piano trio performing outside the A la Carte restaurant. They included popular Scottish violinist John "Jock" Hume; cellist Percy Taylor; and pianist John Woodward. Hartley and White Star's musical director had hand-picked them all, recruiting some from rival Cunarders; both Brailey and Bricoux had most recently played aboard *Carpathia*.

For reasons of economy, White Star did not sign *Titanic*'s musicians as crew but as second class passengers. That grasping contingency would, for a period of time, deprive their widows and children of benefits distributed from the crew's General *Titanic* Fund. But at least the terms of their contracts restricted their shipboard obligations to producing music only; Hamburg-America's bandsmen of the period had to polish brass between gigs.

Aboard *Olympic*-class ships, a novel Reception Room anticipated the vessels' main dining room, duplicating the palm courts gracing every metropolitan, seaside, or spa hotel. It embraced the final descent of the main staircase and, occupying the hull's width, served as perfect before and after meal rendezvous. Comfortable chairs, potted palms, attentive stewards, and appealing music created an irresistible way station for passengers on their way to or from the dining room. The dispensation of aperitifs before meals and brandy or liqueurs afterward created, in effect, the North Atlantic's first cocktail lounge.

Its existence began to erode ocean liners' hidebound preprandial segregation. Before dinner aboard earlier *Adriatic*, for example, men habitually gravitated to the masculine camaraderie of the Smoking Room. But on *Olympic* and *Titanic* they tended to forsake that macho snuggery for a public room that also welcomed their wives. One huge attraction of that venue was Hartley's quintet. That they regularly played there rather than in the main lounge betrays White Star's new sociomusical strategy.

At thirty-three, leader Wallace Henry Hartley was tall, slim, and self-effacing with a well-brushed head of brown hair. He had grown up in a dedicated musical environment. His father, Albion, was choirmaster of the Bethel Independent Methodist Church in the Lancashire town of Colne. Wallace sang in the choir, as did his older sister Mary Ellen; both children studied the violin.

Young Wallace's first job was as bank clerk but, predictably, music took over his life almost at once. He played violin for the Harrogate Spa reception room and was subsequently promoted to conductor of the Bridlington orchestra; thereafter, he toured extensively with the Carl Rosa and Moody-Manners opera companies.

Then the sea beckoned and, for more than eighty voyages, Hartley sailed first as violinist and later bandmaster aboard *Lusitania* and then *Mauretania*. A good sailor, he throve on shipboard. Such was his reputation that, in the spring of 1912, White Star's musical director offered him the post of bandmaster aboard *Titanic*, a coveted appointment for which Hartley was, by then, eminently well qualified.

The only disadvantage of White Star rather than Cunard employment was geographical, distressing not only his family but, even more acutely, his Leeds fiancée, Maria Robinson. Brief, convenient commutes between Lancashire and Liverpool would be a thing of the past as longer train journeys separating Southampton from the Midlands would mean shorter home time between crossings.

Regardless, Hartley deemed the offer irresistible. *Titanic* was larger, grander, and more prestigious than either Cunard flier and how flattering to be awarded the post. After a flurry of exchanged telegrams, he departed for Southampton at the last minute on 9 April, the day before *Titanic* sailed.

Wallace Hartley was by then not only a dapper and accomplished director, he also had profited from years of observing and rubbing shoulders with first class passengers. A quick social study, the young impresario began to outfit himself with the gewgaws and appurtenances of the gentry, adopting the swank veneer of transatlantic regular, rather than provincial naïf from Colne.

His deft orchestrations for violin, viola, cello, bass, and piano rewarded passengers with a lilting cornucopia. More than just a leader with a baton, Hartley embraced multiple responsibilities—librarian, arranger, conductor, and, always, performer. That last role was pivotal because his was the ensemble's only violin, the lead instrument that habitually carried the melodic line.

Because the Reception Room boasted a dance floor, Hartley's music had to include more than traditional palm court fare, a requirement that came with the transatlantic territory. Shipboard's musical sophistication surpassed the ambition of Britain's average repertoire, largely because of its pervasive American admixture. In addition to rehearsing, playing, and conducting, Hartley had to be au courant with the latest uptempo fads that American passenger couples requested. To maintain better contacts with both his music director and colleagues on either shore, Hartley selected the apt and apropos cable address HOTLEY.

New York was the source of some revolutionary new music. And the moment ragtime invaded midocean lounges, operatic overtures and operetta medleys no longer sufficed; selections by Puccini, Lehár, Romberg, and Herbert had to be augmented by new rhythms and new names, prime among them that of young Irving Berlin.

During Manhattan turnarounds, Hartley eschewed the taverns and oyster houses favored by his shipmates. Instead, he prowled Tin Pan Alley, on the qui vive for the latest music. He searched out performers, composers, publishers and, always, precious sheet music. A backlog of selections already dragooned aboard Cunarders included "The Gollywog's Cakewalk," "Grizzly Bear," and, inevitably, the wildly popular "Alexander's Ragtime Band." Rather than soothe, these American numbers tended to agitate, displacing traditional palm court gentility with jazzy syncopation.

By 1912, to replicate that new musical idiom effectively, string ensembles needed instrumental buttressing; the only percussion at Hartley's command was the thump of Ted Brailey's piano. Nevertheless, Hartley improvised. With neither rhythm section, snares, traps, nor bassist Clarke yet slapping his strings, Hartley set bass and cello bows sawing contrapuntally for syncopation. So, too, alternating between interweaving traditional harmonies, his violin and Krins's viola plucked pizzicato descants throughout their upper registers. Determined to respond to all passenger preferences, Hartley embraced the new while still cherishing the old. He kept one eye on the dance floor and the other on his men, sustaining a relentlessly infectious tempo. Player/leaders of small orchestras have to perform and conduct simultaneously, their bowed downbeat an extension of built-in body English; every rhythmic shrug of Hartley's shoulders kept his quintet's output bright and bouncy.

Yet whatever his midocean sophistication, Hartley never relinquished childhood values. On their only Sunday morning aboard *Titanic*, he and his men renounced two-steps for hymns accompanying divine service in the main lounge. Brailey pedaled a harmonium and the players' strings were muted. Most evocative, of course, was midocean's Sunday standard, the Royal Navy hymn "Eternal Father, Strong to Save."

Cellist Elwind Moody, one of Hartley's musician shipmates for twenty-two crossings aboard *Mauretania*, recalled that he once asked Wallace what he would do if he were on a sinking ship.

"I don't think I could do better," responded the choirmaster's son, "than play 'O God, Our Help in Ages Past.'"

Hartley and his entire musical aggregation played together only once, on the last night of their lives. After redundant pianist Jack Woodward dropped out, the seven remaining were mustered by purser McElroy in the main lounge after the collision, in hopes of perpetuating a reassuring, business-as-usual facade.

Later, clad in overcoats and life preservers, they played at the top of the main staircase and then continued their music out on deck, gathered in the open air at the port side entry forward. There was a convenient jog within the 30-inch raised platform of public room ceilings projecting up from the deck below. In his *Titanic* film, director James Cameron stationed his filmic bandsmen out along Boat Deck's railing, but there they would have obstructed traffic badly. Hartley's inboard choice against the gymnasium wall removed his players from what was to become an increasingly hectic paseo.

String selections played in the open air were easily overpowered by increasing commotion, distorting or obscuring the acoustics. Paradoxically, lifeboat occupants some distance away could hear the band clearly while some on deck perceived nothing. Brian Mainwaring, a White Star officer who sailed aboard *Majestic* and *Olympic* in the 1920s, maintained that both Pitman and Lightoller told him they never heard Hartley's men play anything, let alone a hymn. In fact, Mainwaring held his musician shipmates in low esteem, his dismissive crew sobriquet "the bloody band."

Carpathia steward Robert Vaughan also put down ship's musicians, characterizing pianist Theodore Brailey and cellist Roger Bricoux, who would drown on *Titanic*, as "big grumblers," always complaining at mealtimes in the second class smoking room. They could not wait for transfer to the new White Star vessel where the food, they anticipated, would be superior and more plentiful.

Forty-three years after the fact, Victorine Chaudanson Perkins insisted that the band's last selection, played just before the moment of sinking, was "Nearer My God to Thee." Even afloat in the water, the ship's American first class barber, August Weikman, said that he heard the same hymn. Already mentioned, as suggested by Walter Lord, there was a rival final tune claimant, Archibald Joyce's popular waltz "Songe d'Automne."

Just as Hartley, when questioned aboard *Mauretania* years earlier, had spontaneously suggested a hymn for sinking, the idea that a hymn had been played aboard *Titanic* was perceived by a grieving public as divinely apropos. To a world transfixed by the band's heroism, a reverential finale seemed mandatory.

Surviving telegrapher Harold Bride, an astute musical witness, strengthens the case for the waltz. While Phillips remained glued to headphones and telegraph key, Bride dashed back and forth to Commodore Smith on the bridge, sometimes shouldering through Boat Deck's crowds and confusion. More than once, he heard Hartley's men playing both a waltz and some ragtime but never any hymn.

Justice of the peace Barkworth, arriving late on Boat Deck, would testify, "I do not wish to detract from the bravery of anybody but I might mention that when I first came on deck, the band was playing a waltz. The next time I passed where the band had been stationed, the members had thrown down their instruments and were not to be seen."

Was there time for a hymn between Barkworth's consecutive encounters? We shall never know. But there was a coda to support Lord's suggestion: aboard Cunard's *Laconia* in 1914, when the ship's orchestra struck up "Songe d'Automne," a woman came out of the audience and asked the bandmaster to desist, advising him tearfully that it was the tune she had heard aboard *Titanic* the night her husband drowned.

First class passenger Mrs. John Murray Brown embroidered the musicians' role, depicting them as a strolling entourage. Her strongest suit clearly not accuracy, she reported that "the *Titanic*'s band marched from deck to deck playing inspiring music, finishing with 'Nearer My God to Thee.' When our boat left the ship, the musicians were still at their instruments, although the water on the deck was knee-deep."

Regardless of passenger Brown's ludicrous exaggeration, the idea that they played for so long conveys a measure of their dedication. Chilled to the bone, engulfed by tragedy, drowning their only prospect, they produced a final paean of humanity, requiem illumining the perilous night. Whether hymn or waltz seems immaterial; the comfort their music provided was consolation of a high order.

Hartley's devotion to duty was equally remarkable. Though McElroy had initially mustered the musicians, the decision to continue playing was Hartley's alone. Improvisation his strongest suit, he filled an emotional void, occupying his men with a task both familiar and useful, an almost automatic orchestral response to focus numbed minds. Doing the same were Thomas Andrews and the chief deck steward, lashing deck chairs together as flotation devices and hurling them over the side that others might live.

Elsewhere along Boat Deck, younger stewards lost any semblance of discipline, skylarking and smoking openly among passengers in defiance of regulations. Not so the musicians. They carried on, ennobling Hartley's posthumous image with an aura of extraordinary compassion. He obviously cared deeply for the men with whose welfare he was charged. Not only a professional leader, Hartley became a spiritual leader as well, shepherd dutifully tending his flock. That he kept them playing, that they played, provided heaven-sent distraction as much for performer as for listener.

Certainly, no other comfort existed. Even had they *not* played, no musician would have survived. Lifeboats denied them had long since departed and getting the collapsibles into the water was proving difficult. Near the end, it was the increasing slope of *Titanic*'s decks rather than an inundation of seawater that ended their performance and they abandoned their instruments, an unusual exigency for professionals but one belying their desperation.

One cannot help but wonder: how did those dismissed musicians fill their final moments? What about the two liberated pianists, for example; though obviously not trying for a lifeboat, did they keep company with their fellows? And when that string sextet fell silent, what did its members do? Flock indoors for warmth after the chill of their outdoor gig? Did they stay together or scatter? Did they try for one of the collapsibles or retreat toward the stern or embrace the inevitable, surrendering to that icy tide engulfing Boat Deck? And what did Hartley do, mingle with other crewmen or remain with his men?

We can never know because every musician perished. When Hartley's body was found it was clad in his dark uniform with green facings, each adorned with the musicians' traditional lyre. Pulled from the sea by crewmen of the cable ship *Mackay Bennett*, seawater had rendered his musician's costume and brown overcoat into what they mistook for an officer's uniform. After its transfer from dory to cable ship, the body was embalmed rather than merely packed in ice. Strapped across Hartley's shoulders was a leather case, full of sheet music rescued from his cabin.

He was brought ashore and laid out in Halifax's makeshift ice-rink morgue. The contents of his pockets betrayed the growing affluence and success of the thirty-three-year-old musician/conductor: a gold fountain pen inscribed W. H. H., a diamond solitaire ring, a silver cigarette case and match safe, a nickel watch attached to a gold chain, and a gold cigar holder. Those surprisingly upscale keepsakes bespeak moneyed well-being that boded well for Hartley's continued advancement.

If not for *Titanic*, what future might he have enjoyed? Certainly, marriage to his beloved Maria, a detached house in Southampton, doubtless some children, more years afloat and possible promotion to White Star's musical director. Yet, by the same token, transfer ashore would deprive him of his two greatest joys, sailing and playing. But a future of any kind was cruelly denied. His fiancée never married: devastated Maria Robinson lived out her Bridlington spinsterhood for twenty-seven lonely years.

After identifying the body, Hartley's father shipped the coffin by rail to Boston and accompanied it back to Liverpool aboard *Arabic*. At his son's funeral, he would lead the Bethel Choir as it sang "Nearer My God to Thee."

The band's exemplary behavior prompted the erection of plaques, tablets, and plinths in concert halls and bandstands around the world. There is one in the Albert Hall and on 19 April 1913, Southampton's Amalgamated Musicians Union funded a Sicilian marble musicians' memorial in the Old Library, destroyed by bombs during World War II. In Boston's Symphony Hall, an inscribed plaque reads:

IN MEMORY OF THE DEVOTED MUSICIANS WHO WERE DROWNED
STILL PLAYING AS THE TITANIC WENT DOWN, 15 APRIL, 1912

A list of their names follows. Even in far-off Australia, two memorials were erected to *Titanic*'s musicians: a handsome bandstand in Ballarat, in the state of Victoria, and another in the outback at Sturt Park, Broken Hill, its only minor flaw a plinth misspelling that lists cellist Bricoux as Bricouk.

For his funeral on 18 May 1912, Hartley's hometown of Colne pulled out all the stops for its suddenly world-famous native son. Every shop was shuttered in tribute as thousands converged from the surrounding countryside. Dozens of musicians joined the cortege. Six marching bands, including the Fifth Battalion East Lancashire Regiment, played Handel's "The Dead March" from *Saul*. The Colne Orchestral Society marched too, as did a detachment of Scouts whose bugler played "The Last Post" at the sloping gravesite.

Not surprisingly, Hartley's headstone, topped by only a draped column, bore musical adornment. Just below the inscription is chiseled an open hymnal, its left-hand page bearing a treble clef with the opening bars of "Nearer My God to Thee." On the facing page are inscribed the hymn's first words. Underscoring the deceased's profession, sculpted into the marble along the base are violin and bow.

The townspeople of Colne did not stop there, however. A substantial memorial was erected on Albert Road. Initially, contributions were solicited for a commemorative drinking fountain. Even though the Firemen's and Crew Memorial on Southampton Common as well as the Belfast Engineers Memorial had originally incorporated drinking fountains, when Colne's monument committee realized, belatedly, that Hartley had met his death by drowning, it agreed to eschew any involvement with water. Instead, they erected a monument topped by an heroic bronze bust. Riding sidesaddle on projecting cornices just below Hartley's likeness were, in reduced scale, two female figures, shrouded chastely in capes and clutching lyres in their hands.

Those two figures were recently detached and stolen, the result of mere wanton destruction or, more likely, souvenir keepsakes; they have been replaced by plastic replicas.

Sadly, *Titanic* memorials all over Great Britain have suffered badly from vandalism, not only Southampton's drinking fountain but also Godalming's elaborate memorial cloister to Jack Phillips, *Titanic*'s senior Marconi telegrapher. One centenary pledge offers hope for its restoration but that will depend, as always, on the availability of perennially scarce municipal funding as well as public donations. At least Phillips's gravestone, carved in the shape of an iceberg, remains unscathed.

At this chapter's opening, I touched on the double tragedies of 1912, *Titanic*'s loss and the death of Scott's polar party. The two events were additionally linked by the choice of artist commissioned to create memorial statues of both the Royal Navy captain Scott and the Merchant Navy captain Edward J. Smith. She was Lady Scott, née Bruce, the explorer's widow, Kathleen, a professional sculptor in her own right. Her doughty bronze tribute to her late husband stands atop a plinth in London's Waterloo Place, an Antarctic stalwart posed resolutely next door to his doomed Arctic forerunner Sir John Franklin. A second casting can be found in New Zealand.

Lady Scott's effigy of Commodore Smith aroused unkinder response. Although it was intended for Smith's birthplace of Stoke-on-Trent, the town fathers, critical of the captain's ruinous speed the night of the sinking, refused to accept the statue. It was erected instead in nearby Lichfield.

Recently, the Lichfield mayoral council offered to underwrite the cost of delivering and reerecting Smith's likeness in Stoke. Once again, the town fathers refused, enmity still rankling a hundred years on. At the time of his death, Smith received a commodore's wage of £1,250 per annum but, not surprisingly, his widow was denied his posthumous £200 annual perquisite, a "non-collision bonus."

In Britain's village of Terwick, near Rogate, an enviable tribute is dedicated to the memory of a *Titanic* passenger: a field full of brightly colored lupine that blooms and thrives each spring, perhaps the ideal memorial, self-perpetuating and presumably vandalproof.

CHAPTER 9

WALTER AT PLAY

I think it is one of the best of your unique series, and at once amused and touched me because you made the situation so convincing. You clearly have a much more light-hearted background than my own.

Excerpt from Leslie Reade letter to Walter Lord, 24 April 1975

No one was more informed, serious, perhaps even reverential about *Titanic* than Walter Lord. But there came a time, on several anniversaries of the vessel's foundering, when he violated that respectful norm with some letters, ostensibly composed on board, that ventured into intriguing parody. To him, *Titanic* was invariably "the old girl," bespeaking a fondness and familiarity typical of these playful pastiches.

These seven letters were addressed to the late Leslie Reade, a London barrister, BBC writer, and *Titanic* historian. Walter and Leslie began corresponding in the 1960s and, over years of shared *Titanic* fascination, became great friends. He and his wife, Judith, lived in London's Ivor Court. Leslie had labored for years on a long manuscript entitled *The Ship That Stood Still*, an exhaustive quasi-polemic about the Leyland Line's *Californian*, the nearby steamship that rendered no assistance to stricken *Titanic* that agonizing April night. Leslie had been trying to get it in print for years with different publishers bracketing the Atlantic: in Cambridge Patrick Stephens and, in Annapolis, America's prestigious Naval Institute. Walter did all he could to help his friend and fellow author, vetting Leslie's typescript for errors and offering specific, constructive suggestions.

Leslie's obsession with *Titanic* rivaled Walter's and had started at a similarly young age. He grew up in South Africa where Reade *père* owned an ostrich farm. It intrigued his eight-year-old son that a shipment of ostrich feathers was among the cargo bound for New

York in the hold of the lost White Star liner. At almost the same age, Walter had been taken by his widowed mother for a transatlantic crossing aboard *Olympic*; from that compelling White Star experience dates the young Baltimorean schoolboy's similarly dedicated fascination with both her and her lost sister ship.

Portions of Reade's manuscript were considered by both publishers as potentially libelous, particularly worrisome in the United Kingdom. Additionally, his documentation was intense. After his first reading, Walter had commented, "What struck me most was the way you examined every argument from both sides: nothing swept under the rug, or ignored as though it didn't exist."

Examining every argument from both sides was all very well but it spawned an often dense, overrich syntax. In truth, Reade had toiled so long and so obsessively on his chapters that they were becoming unmanageable; regardless, he adamantly refused to cut a single word.

Walter's seven extant anniversary letters appear here in print for the first time. Their copyright was held by the late Edward De Groot, esteemed Dutch journalist, broadcaster, author, wireless authority, and *Titanic* expert. Edward's initial contact with Walter occurred as the result of a New York interview he did for Dutch radio in March 1972. He and Walter became good friends, their mutual hobbyhorse, yet again, White Star's lost vessel. Fifteen years later, De Groot wrote a well-received anniversary volume, called in Dutch 75 *Jaar Titanic* (75 Years of *Titanic*); it was published by De Alk and would reappear nine years later with a different, simpler title, *Titanic*.

It was, fittingly, De Groot who would finally usher *The Ship That Stood Still* into print in 1993 for Patrick Stephens, four years after Leslie Reade died of old age. He did something that the author had consistently refused to do: pruned the manuscript skillfully. Approving that vital editing chore was his widow, Judith Reade.

Although Walter may never have anticipated that these letters to Leslie would be published, Edward and I felt that he would have doubtless enjoyed seeing them. They not only offer a glimpse of his highly amusing and inventive turn of mind, they also capitalize on the presence of an occasionally naive but consummately observant *Titanic* passenger.

One can evaluate *Titanic*'s social mores on many levels, from the most sophisticated to the banal. Banality usually wins out. By and large, most of the public and even some contemporary historians seem content to be dazzled, cherishing life aboard the lost liner as adulation of the Edwardian establishment. That maiden voyage crowd, they imply, conformed happily to Robin Leach's television series *Lifestyles of the Rich and Famous*, broadcast in the 1980s and '90s. Hallmarks of every episode included snobbism, idleness, and unbridled extravagance, pandering to the cult of celebrity that has become, alas, our never-ending global obsession.

Walter's *Titanic* take was more discerning. However rich or famous, he depicted the vessel's upper crust as essentially vulnerable human beings. Affluence or status notwithstanding, they were subject to the same behavioral shortcomings exhibited by every shipmate, whether immigrant or industrialist. Not for Walter *Titanic*'s social clichés; he reveals instead a first class of the sometimes tiresome, jockeying, or boring, who would become ensnared in the retrospective glare of maritime history. His telling vignettes cut *Titanic*'s passenger profiles down to size, delineating them as the archetypal shipboard occupants they undoubtedly were.

Walter must have been pleased with his consecutive indulgences to Leslie because they exhibited such annual refinement. But they stopped, suddenly and inexplicably, after the best of the lot had been posted in 1976; no more would emerge from that inspired typewriter.

Shortly afterward, by coincidence, an unnamed correspondent who knew about the letters sent Walter a parody of his own. It was rejected briefly but firmly: "Good ideas," he responded cursorily, "are always copied. Best, Walter." Walter must have either felt he had exhausted the genre or just wished to get on with other matters. But the verdict "good ideas" suggests to me unmistakable authorial satisfaction with his achievement.

His first missive was typed in 1969, dated 14 April, the anniversary's eve. It will help to know that Clarence Moore was an insufferable *Titanic* raconteur, brimful of hoary anecdotes with which he bored every passenger within earshot.

Dear Leslie—

It's a little after 1:00 A.M., and I've just passed through the smoking room, where Archie Butt, Frank D. Millet, Clarence Moore, and another man were sitting quietly around a table. It occurred to me that they wanted to show their entire indifference to the danger.

"Have any of you seen Leslie Reade?" I asked. They all shook their heads, and Moore began relating one of his anecdotes about the time he interviewed the outlaw Captain Anse Hatfield. I wandered out on deck and ran into Lightoller, Dr. O'Loughlin, Dr. Simpson, and two of the pursers. They were standing in a group shaking hands.

"Have any of you seen Leslie Reade?" I asked. They too said no. Attracted by the sound of pistol shots, I went to the rail and saw Fifth Officer Lowe brandishing his revolver as Boat 14 dropped down toward the sea.

"Have *you* seen Leslie Reade?" I asked. Lowe shook his head, then observed that someone did get into his boat with a woman's shawl over his head. Could that have been Leslie Reade?

Certainly not! But there's not much more time. The lights are beginning to glow red; and in some deck pantry I can hear crockery breaking. I think I'll just put this in a bottle and hurl it into the sea, hoping that it finds you alive and well. You've been unusually silent, but I trust that means you've been unusually busy, not that you've failed to get the odds and ends I've sent your way the last month or two. I especially liked the *Queen Mary* as a one-stacker.

When you get a chance, let me know how you are, what you think of the Marcus book, what sort of reception it has had, and how you're getting along in your own various endeavors. As advance payment, I'm enclosing my long-promised collation.

Best,

Walter

[handwritten] P.S. Your letter of April 11 has just arrived! Since this was already typed and I'm quite pleased with it, I'm mailing it anyhow. Will write again in a week or so. Best to Judith —W.

This first letter, unlike any to follow, was a hybrid, part jest and part serious, fantasy intermingled with the nuts and bolts of their normal correspondence. In the midst of his penultimate paragraph, just after Walter has "hurled his note into the sea," the charade ends abruptly and he turns to contemporary matters, wondering about Leslie's silence and his reaction to some already posted items. He is anxious for Leslie's evaluation of Geoffrey Marcus's *Maiden Voyage*, published in 1969. The nature of his "collation" is not revealed.

Titanic's two Irish surgeons—principal William O'Loughlin and subordinate John Edward Simpson—as well as Lightoller and some junior pursers, strolled *Titanic*'s boat deck to inspire confidence among increasingly distraught passengers, displaying a fortitude they may not have felt but wished to convey. As the only survivor among them, Lightoller had obviously shared the moment. Walter cites that almost-forgotten episode to buttress the haunting reality on which he grounded his fantasies.

The crew was devoted to both doctors. Stewardess Mary Sloan had shared a dram of whiskey with Simpson earlier that night. Terrified, she wondered aloud what was going to happen.

"Child," he replied, "things are very bad."

Fifth officer Harold Lowe fired off two warning pistol shots to deter interlopers from rushing lifeboat no. 14. The words he actually shouted after his fusillade were: "If anyone else tries to board, this is what he will get!"

Next year's jape indicates that Walter, having refined the form, was now wholeheartedly immersed in charade. All the remaining letters contain not one genuine word.

April 14
7:30 P.M.

Dear Leslie—

This is short and quick because I don't want Mr. Gatti to see me. I'm sure he'd never approve my writing letters in his beautiful Louis Seize restaurant. It is now 7:30, and the diners are drifting in. As Colonel Gracie puts it, "On these occasions full dress is always *en règle*."

Almost hidden in an alcove I can see the Wideners greeting Captain Smith for dinner. The Carters and the Thayers are also at the table; and, oh yes, there's Archie Butt too. Behind me those dreadful Duff Gordons are sitting, and nearby are Mr. and Mrs. Harris—something seems to me to be the matter with her arm. Dr. O'Loughlin is here too, and Bruce Ismay has just joined him.

Funny thing, I passed both Ismay and the Captain on the way down, just outside the smoke room. The Captain called him over (that doesn't often happen!), and Ismay gave him some sort of piece of paper.

Enough of this prattle. Just wanted you to know that all is well, and that we're having a splendid, if uneventful trip. Best,

Walter

Inspired prattle, indeed! Walter casts himself as ingenuously trying to evade the scrutiny of A la Carte Manager Luigi Gatti. Not only is Walter not in black tie, he is also using one of the restaurant's coveted tables as a surreptitious writing desk. Where was Walter actually seated? Not out in the staircase entry but, he suggests, "hidden in an alcove," of which there were none. Whatever his vantage point, he has a bird's-eye view of the evening's A la Carte crowd, including the Wideners' dinner party, the guest list for which included Captain Smith, Archie Butt, and the Philadelphian Carters and Thayers.

He takes a gratuitous swipe at Scottish Bart, Sir Cosmo and Lady Duff Gordon, the couple who, at 1 A.M. the following morning, would abandon *Titanic* in the no. 1 emergency boat. Designed to hold forty, it contained only twelve, as though a private yacht. Aboard were both Duff Gordons, Lady Duff Gordon's maid Miss Francatelli, two Americans, seven cooperative stokers, and several suitcases. When the crewmen complained that their pay stopped after *Titanic* sank, Sir Cosmo impulsively if foolishly presented each with a signed IOU for £5, which, in devastating hindsight, suggested bribes to discourage embarking additional passengers.

Broadway impresario Henry Harris and his wife, Renée, were familiar figures aboard *Titanic* and something was indeed "the matter with her arm." That afternoon, while descending the main staircase and slipping on an inadvertently dropped cream tart, she fell and broke some bones, a nasty compound elbow fracture. Dr. O'Loughlin had put on a cast after it had been expertly set with the assistance of passenger Dr. Henry Frauenthal, an American orthopedic surgeon fortuitously on board.

Earlier, passenger Lord had spied White Star's managing director Bruce Ismay handing Captain Smith a Marconigram warning of ice in *Titanic*'s path; he could not resist another parenthetical swipe, pointing up the uneasy enmity separating the two. Prior to their meeting, first class passenger Emily Ryerson had encountered Ismay brandishing the same message. He had confided portentously, "We have just had news that we are in amongst the icebergs."

"Of course, you will slow down," cautioned Mrs. Ryerson.

"Oh, no," Ismay retorted. "We will put on more boilers and get out of it!"

Their exchange bears pertinently on apportioning *Titanic* blame. Did Ismay urge Smith to maintain speed or was he, as subsequently claimed, merely a passenger subservient to the captain's wishes? Assessing his role, coupled with the fact of his opportunistic survival, would become irresistible grist for every reporter's mill.

The following year's letter was supposedly written on the afternoon of the fourteeth, nine hours before the iceberg's appearance. In it, we share the inevitable end-of-voyage letdown triggered by distribution of baggage declaration forms. It is all there—shipboard's mood of anticipatory regret as the crossing approaches its end and its still unwitting climax.

At sea
3:30 P.M. April 14

Dear Leslie—

It's getting so cold outside I thought I'd come in and write you a letter, but I'm afraid it's going to be brief, for all the writing bureaus are taken with people filling out their baggage declaration forms. Right now I'm settled in a cozy chair, pleasantly eaves-dropping on a conversation between two young American ladies who seem to be shipboard acquaintances. One of them is wearing a pair of pince-nez, and I can't help wondering who told her that made her look attractive!

Mr. Hoffman's two little boys are playing in the enclosed deck just outside, and that American kinematograph photographer and his French wife (think you pointed them out to me at Southampton) are also nearby. How fascinating it will be to have a complete film record of this maiden voyage.

You'll be interested to hear that there's a motor engineer on board who has invented a new carburetter [*sic*] which he thinks will be important to automobiling. He is taking a model of it to Detroit to show the investors there. Here he is, the simplest and most unknown of men, and just suppose that his invention—known at the moment only to himself—should revolutionize the whole industry!

Wonders never cease as the world, like this giant vessel, moves steadily toward an ever brighter future.

Best, Walter

The pince-nez lady was surviving first class passenger Gretchen Longley of Hudson, New York. More famous are the two hapless Navratil children. Their father, traveling under the alias Hoffman, had abducted them from his estranged Parisian wife and was spiriting them to America. But like too many best-laid plans involving *Titanic*, things went tragically awry: he would drown and ascertaining the identity of two unattached French waifs would prove a thorny conundrum for *Carpathia*'s purser.

We have already met American cinematographer William Harbeck, traveling not with his wife but his Parisian mistress, Henriette Yvois. Alas for the hopes and dreams of the (mythical) "carburetter" inventor bound for Detroit. Walter's closing paragraph spins a telling riff about the future's boundless scientific promise. Privy to the tragedy about to ensue, we can but admire his plangent irony.

In his next letter, Walter visits the Boat Deck's radio room. It was apparently part of passenger Lord's ubiquitous privilege that he could penetrate every space on board, both public and private.

April 14
11:39 P.M.

Dear Leslie—

About a half-hour ago I stopped by the wireless room to send you greetings from mid-ocean, but Mr. Phillips seemed so overworked, I decided to drop you this line instead. At the time, Phillips was trying to relay congratulations from a chap named Reade to an American named Lord, whose book had been selected by the Book-of-the-Month Club, when some nearby ship broke in. I don't blame Phillips for telling the other operator to "shut up." Reade's message struck me as being so gracious it deserved priority over anything else.

Now I'm snuggled in a sheltered corner of the Boat Deck, writing by the light of the gymnasium windows. The voyage has been splendid. The ship is a virtual floating town, although out here in the dark, under those four great funnels reaching up toward the stars, I suddenly feel very much alone. That is, I did feel alone until just a second ago, when the crow's-nest bell clanged three times, reminding me that there are others too out here in the dark, shepherding us safely and swiftly toward shore.

Must go in now; it's getting colder and colder.

Hastily, Walter

Reference is made to Jack Phillips here for the first time. The senior Marconi operator, he did not survive, though subordinate Harold Bride did. But the junior telegrapher was not present when Walter stopped by; he was probably just waking up in their sleeping cabin next door.

There was, in fact, no need for Walter to enter the wireless room; he easily could have dispatched his cable from the purser's desk. But by being on hand, he could quote verbatim Phillips's response to an interruption from *Californian*'s telegrapher Cyril Evans. In that, alas, solitary exchange, which took place just after 11 P.M., Evans's helpful advisory about ice had annoyed Phillips who, burdened with a backlog of urgent passenger traffic, cut off the Leyland Line Marconi man ruthlessly.

Rather than cabling Reade, Walter decides to write him a letter instead. The spectacle of *Titanic*'s funnel quartet towering into the night sky contributes to an awareness of others sharing his vigil. When, at exactly 11:40, he hears three strokes from the crow's nest bell, every *Titanic* buff will experience an undeniable frisson of apprehension, realizing that the clangor was not, as Lord blithely assumes, a tocsin of reassurance but an ominous harbinger of impact, lookout Frederick Fleet's belated iceberg sighting.

A year later, 1973's letter is a grumpy litany of complaint. Passenger Lord has had enough of inefficiency and indifference, voicing almost prissy affectation and disappointment.

At sea,
April 14, 11:50 P.M.

Dear Leslie—

This dreadful boat! I can't imagine why I took it, except you urged me to, and you've never given me a piece of bad advice.

Anyhow, we no sooner started from Southampton when we almost collided with the *New York*. Then we nearly ran aground in Queenstown, or at least it looked that way, judging from all the mud we stirred up.

And you know how I hate to complain, but nothing seems to be shipshape. Imanita Shelley tells me that her stewardess can't even get a tray to serve her breakfast, and that nice Mrs. Parrish of Kentucky tells me that the ladies' toilet on her deck doesn't even have all its fixtures installed yet. I also hear that the restaurant galley hot press broke down today, and I simply can't stand the color of the pebble dashing on my private promenade deck. Much too dark.

The strain has been so much that I went down for a massage this afternoon, and Mrs. Slocomb tells me that the Turkish Bath too has had its troubles. The builders left the place a mess—empty beer bottles all about. Shocking.

Now something has happened again. We have suddenly stopped and are simply drifting about in the middle of the ocean! Steward Johnson thinks we've dropped a propeller blade.

It's all too exasperating. I promise you one thing: this is the last time I shall ever take *Titanic*.

Best, Walter

Here, passenger Lord unburdens himself of an atypical, self-indulgent tirade. In the process, he inadvertently imparts his cabin location. Not surprisingly, he chose one of the two best on board, a grand B Deck suite with two adjoining staterooms, private bath, and a sitting room complete with faux fireplace. They were exactly the kind of lavish quarters that someone of his pretension and clout would like to have booked. (In fact, the other one was occupied by Bruce Ismay.) Describing his private promenade overlooking the sea with its too-dark "pebble dashing," he has borrowed one of Thomas Andrews's inspection notes, a renovation to be passed along for remedy to Harland and Wolff's decorative staff.

Imanita Shelley and her mother had found their second class cabin woefully incomplete, its plumbing fixtures not hooked up. Maud Slocombe—"Sloky" to crew intimates—was one of the company's first female masseuses. She was furious about the squalid condition in which Belfast workmen had left her Turkish bath. Because of their neglect, the space could not open for business until day three of the crossing, curtailing Mrs. Slocomb's potential tip income.

Steward Johnson's analysis of a thrown propeller blade was a consistent crew reaction to *Titanic*'s 11:40 shudder. *Olympic* had shed a blade at sea the year previous and more than one crewman made a similar assumption that night.

Like every passenger since time immemorial, Lord's spirits vary from day to day. His next letter, written for 1975's anniversary, makes for a telling contrast with his unhappiness and ennui of the previous letter. Herewith, Walter as gambler rather than grumbler.

At sea,
April 14
11:55 P.M.

Dear Leslie—

I've just had the most wonderful bit of luck! This afternoon I met a charming American named Jay Yates. He was most friendly, and tonight after dinner he invited me to join himself and a couple of companions in the smoke room for a friendly game of the new "contract bridge." I felt most flattered to be asked after knowing him such a short time.

We began playing for ten cents a point and while that seemed quite high to me, Mr. Yates pointed out that it was only cards and things usually evened out in the end. Well, I won a little at first, but then my luck really turned against me. Mr. Clarence Moore was recounting some of his adventures at the next table, and I suppose I just couldn't concentrate. Anyhow, about a half hour ago I was down some 4,000 points.

Then I simply got a wonderful hand. Diamonds were trumps, and I had the king, jack, nine, seven, maybe two or three more, and the way my partner acted, I felt sure he must have the rest. I opened by bidding three diamonds, and to my surprise Mr. Yates doubled. I of course redoubled, although I hated to take advantage of him. But before I could start playing my hand, the ship gave the strangest shudder and came to a stop.

Mr. Yates and the others went out on deck to see what had happened, but it was too cold for me; so I just waited for them to come back and go on with the game. When they did come back, Mr. Yates was very nervous, and without so much as an explanation, said the game was over and he was going down to his cabin. He and the others simply left me there holding this marvelous hand!

Well, I thought what rotten luck, but before putting the cards away, I glanced at the hand he had thrown down, and do you know, he had the ace, queen, ten, and all the other diamonds in the deck! Why, he would have taken the hand after all, and I would have lost far more money than I could possibly afford.

So in a flash, my bad luck changed to good, and I thought I'd write you about it before turning in. The ship is still stopped, but with the splendid stroke of good fortune I enjoyed tonight, I can't imagine anything but smooth sailing the rest of the way to New York.

Best, Walter

This letter prompted an appreciative response from Leslie, excerpted in this chapter's epigraph. Jay Yates (his real name probably R. H. Rogers) was a professional gambler, one of the "boatmen" who made their living bilking gullible passengers. He and his ilk were not only masters at manipulating cards, they were also charmers who lured suckers like Walter into games they could ill afford. Their smooth come-on after only the briefest introduction was classic boatman strategy, completely lost on Walter the naïf.

On this occasion, Yates and his confederates played in the smoking room. In fact, crooked gamblers seldom plied their trade in public, risking exposure by the pursers; they preferred fleecing victims in the privacy of a large suite, sine qua non for prudent boatmen. Walter, a bridge neophyte, was initially reluctant to play, nervous about the possible stakes. (Given his cabin's location and expense, one would have thought him safe from financial worry.)

Apparently, that night in the smoking room, caution reigned. Suddenly deep in the hole, Walter was astonished when his diamond bid was redoubled by Yates and even more astonished to discover, after *Titanic*'s strange shudder and Yates's departure, that his opponent's discarded hand held more diamonds than his.

What a relief that the game had ended so fortuitously, transporting Walter with delight. That last-minute reprieve puts him in an exuberant frame of mind about the balance of the crossing.

Yates, incidentally, did not survive and left a scribbled note that a fellow passenger was asked to deliver to a sister somewhere in Ohio. No Yates appears on any *Titanic* passenger manifest; either the man drowned or, thanks to one final con, he managed to expunge his identity permanently.

The 1976 letter contains Walter's most outrageously amusing charade, the carefully drawn fop at his fumbling best. The episode features a beautiful and seductive wife, an illicit cabin rendezvous, an opportunistic embrace, cuckoldry of her unseen but obviously suspicious husband, and, overall, complete disregard of *Titanic*'s plight. It makes for a seamlessly crafted and utterly hilarious finale.

At sea
April 15
12:15 A.M.

Dear Leslie—

What a narrow escape! It all began while I was listening to the orchestra tonight at after-dinner coffee. It has been a subject both of observation and admiration that there are so many beautiful women aboard, but surely the loveliest of them all was sitting at the next table. She smiled at me, and I was just about to introduce myself when up came that bloody bore Colonel Gracie, circulating as he always does on these occasions.

Well, by the time he left, she was gone too, but there on my table was a little unsigned note that said simply, "B-78, 11:40." I knocked at the appointed hour. She let me in; we embraced. . . . Leslie, there has never been an embrace like it. When that girl kissed me, the whole ship seemed to quiver, and I swear I felt the deck sway under my feet!

There we stood locked in each other's arms, I don't know how long. I can only say time seemed to stand still. Under the spell of her love, even the engines seemed to stop running.

Then suddenly, there was a knock on the door. I couldn't imagine who it was, and asked, "What is it?" She, gorgeous creature, was plainly irritated and said, "Tell us what the trouble is." A voice said it was Steward Etches and we were to come on deck.

At midnight? A likely story! Of course we refused, and after some more knocking, whoever it was went away. But I was petrified. I felt certain it wasn't the steward at all, but probably her husband. Having failed to trick me into opening the door, he had undoubtedly gone to get the Master-At-Arms.

Frantically I adjusted my tie and dashed out. Fortunately, there is a gents room almost across the corridor, and I ducked into one of the booths. I'm now "sitting it out," until I'm sure the coast is clear.

From the sound of things, that may take a while. Her husband seems to have aroused the whole ship! So until things quiet down, I've decided to while away the time by jotting you this letter. Strange, I never even learned the damsel's name, but as I said at the start, what a narrow escape!

Best,

Walter

Walter Lord's parodies remain a tour de force that not one of his fellow historians has ever conceived or attempted, another of the man's imperishable *Titanic* legacies.

BIBLIOGRAPHY

Beavis, Debbie. *Who Sailed on Titanic?* Hersham, UK: Ian Allan Publishing, 2002.

Beesley, Lawrence. *The Loss of S.S. Titanic*. Boston: Houghton Mifflin, 1912.

Bisset, Sir James. *Tramps and Ladies*. New York: Criterion Books, 1959.

Booth, John, and Sean Coughlan. *Titanic, Signals of Disaster*. Westbury, UK: White Star Publications, 1993.

Bullock, Shan F. *A Titanic Hero, Thomas Andrews, Shipbuilder*. Riverside, CT: 7 C's Press, 1973.

Davie, Michael. *The Titanic: The Full Story of the Tragedy*. London: The Bodley Head, 1986.

Eaton, John P., and Charles A. Haas. *Titanic, Triumph and Tragedy*. London: Patrick Stephens, 1986, 1994.

Flayhart, William Henry III. *The American Line*. New York: W. W. Norton, 2000.

Gillespie, Vera, and John Gillespie. *The "Titanic Man" Carlos F. Hurd*. Grover, MO: 1996.

Howse, Christopher. *How We Saw It, 150 Years of* The Daily Telegraph, *1855–2005*. London: Ebury Press, 2004.

Jolly, W. P. *Marconi*. London: Constable and Company, 1972.

Jones, Nicolette. *The Plimsoll Sensation*. Boston: Little, Brown, 2006.

de Kerbreck, Richard. *Ships of the White Star Line*. Hersham, UK: Ian Allan Publishing, 2009.

Lawrence, Jenny. *The Way it Was: Walter Lord on his Life and Books*. New York: 2009.

Lord, Walter. *A Night to Remember*. New York: Henry Holt and Company, 1955.

——— *The Night Lives On*. New York: William Morrow and Company, 1986.

Marconi, Degna. *My Father, Marconi*. Ottawa: Baltimore Book Publishing, 1982.

Marcus, Geoffrey. *The Maiden Voyage*. London: George Allen and Unwin, 1969.

Matsen, Brad. *Titanic's Last Secrets*. New York: Twelve, 2008.

Maxtone-Graham, John. *The Only Way to Cross*. New York: Macmillan, 1972.

McCluskie, Tom. *No Place for a Boy*. Stroud, UK: The History Press, 2009.

——— *Harland & Wolff*. London: Conway Maritime Press, 1998.

Moss, Michael, and John R. Hume. *Shipbuilders to the World*. Belfast: The Blackstaff Press, 1986.

Priestley, J. B. *The Edwardians*. London: William Heinemann, 1970.

Rankin, Nicholas. *A Genius for Deception*. New York: Oxford University Press, 2008.

Reade, Leslie. *The Ship That Stood Still*. ed. Edward P. De Groot. London: Patrick Stephens, 1993.

Rostron, Sir Arthur H. *Home from the Sea*. New York: Macmillan, 1931.

Thayer, John B. *The Sinking of the S.S. Titanic*. Philadelphia: privately printed, 1940.

Wade, Wyn Craig. *The Titanic: End of a Dream*. New York: Rawson, Wade, 1979.

Watson, Arnold, and Betty Watson. *Roster of Valor*. Riverside, CT: 7C's Press, 1984.

INDEX

JOHN MAXTONE-GRAHAM has written numerous works; his first, *The Only Way to Cross* of 1972 remains "the bible of the ship buffs." Among many others to follow were *Titanic Survivor*, *Safe Return Doubtful*, and, most recently, the definitive *Normandie* and *France/Norway*. He currently spends more than half his year lecturing aboard cruise ships and makes his home on Manhattan's Upper West Side.